The Human Face of Globalization

The Human Face of Globalization

From Multicultural to Mestizaje

Jacques Audinet

Translated from the
French by
Frances Dal Chele

ROWMAN & LITTLEFIELD PUBLISHERS, INC.
Lanham • Boulder • New York • Toronto • Oxford

ROWMAN & LITTLEFIELD PUBLISHERS, INC.

Published in the United States of America
by Rowman & Littlefield Publishers, Inc.
A wholly owned subsidiary of The Rowman & Littlefield Publishing Group, Inc.
4501 Forbes Boulevard, Suite 200, Lanham, Maryland 20706
www.rowmanlittlefield.com

PO Box 317
Oxford
OX2 9RU, UK

British Library Cataloguing in Publication Information Available

Library of Congress Cataloging-in-Publication Data

Audinet, Jacques.
 [Temps du métissage. English]
 The human face of globalization : from multicultural to mestizaje / Jacques
Audinet ; translated from the French by Frances Dal Chele.
  p. cm.
 Includes bibliographical references and index.
 ISBN 0-7425-4227-0 (hardcover : alk. paper)—ISBN 0-7425-4228-9 (pbk. :
alk. paper)
 1. Miscegenation. 2. Multiculturalism. 3. Acculturation. I. Title.

 GN254.A8313 2004
 306—dc22
                          2004017876

Printed in the United States of America

♾™ The paper used in this publication meets the minimum requirements of
American National Standard for Information Sciences—Permanence of Paper
for Printed Library Materials, ANSI/NISO Z39.48-1992.

~

Contents

~

Introduction
Encounters . . .

Mestizo. The word is gradually finding its way into places and situations where previously it was unknown. It no longer solely concerns other people, elsewhere, on islands; now it concerns us, here. It no longer implies journeys to faraway places, it describes what is happening on our doorstep. The neighborhoods of our cities have become mestizo. So have music, education, and information. People are beginning to talk about *mestizaje* in connection with ideas, groups, or lifestyles.

Ten years ago, even five, in France the words *mestizo* or *mestizaje* were never heard in everyday conversations. They were limited to the fancies of a few poets or reserved for use by a restricted number of specialists and their assistants, those who were familiar with history and devoted to studying the immense changes that European expansion, starting in the sixteenth century, inflicted upon the inhabitants of the New World.

Whenever the words are used in the course of everyday conversation, they designate something very precise as defined in dictionaries: *mestizaje* means a mix of two different races. Everyone has encountered a mestizo at one time or another, while traveling or in their family's past. It might be that an ancestor had sailed the seas, creating unexpected cousins, or perhaps a soldier had come back with a beautiful foreign bride. In any case, *mestizaje* necessarily happened far away; it was

1

a leftover from other times and places, an aftermath of colonialist expansion. In short, it was an accident, a localized disturbance in the sure stream of our alliances. It was more amusing than troubling because it was exotic. It aroused curiosity because it was strange and unexpected. *Mestiizaje is* rather fascinating too—Pierre Loti's novels or the opera *Madame Butterfly* owe to it their success—but also a source of anxiety, because it is a risky thing: we are never sure of what the unknown can produce. In short, it was nice to contemplate from a safe distance, without taking any personal risks.

Nevertheless, the reality existed long before the word. *Mestizaje* has been the focus of renewed attention over the past several years because it names what already exists. What is spreading is not the word but a certain reality: encounter, mixing, the interaction of people of different origins, languages, lifestyles, colors, and—let's use the word for now— races. Sociologists prudently use the word *intercultural* to describe this reality, while ordinary language uses the *mixing of the races* and *mestizaje.* The fact that the word is being used more frequently is evidence of a heightened awareness that our societies have become pluralistic and multiethnic to an extent never before seen in the history of humanity.

Mestizaje is a reality for which we were scarcely prepared. A visionary like Charles de Gaulle could proclaim: "*Mestizaje* is the future," but for many people, the matter never crossed their mind. Now the question is definitely on the agenda, and for everyone. Almost every family has its across-the-border marriage. Not only travel but our daily life places us in contact with other people, people radically different from us and yet with whom our lives are destined to intertwine and commingle.

As a result of this widespread reality, trying to redefine *mestizaje* poses some problems. Formerly reserved for the exotic, now the word is increasingly common and no longer uniquely applies to individuals, but to groups, languages, lifestyles, clothing, food, even religions—in short, *cultural mestizaje.* Is such an extended meaning legitimate? Might it be an improvement?

What does this word designate now and what does it connote? Even more important, what does the fact that it is showing up in the most unexpected areas signify? That the word is broadening is all the more reason to try to determine everything it conveys. The partial goal of the following pages is just that: to specify just what *mestizaje* means today.

I encountered *mestizaje* outside of Europe. Thought it was something that concerned other people, it was something that, strangely enough, didn't leave me indifferent; it left me out, or made me a stranger to a reality that existed independently of me and didn't need me to exist. I remember my arrival at the airport in Rio and my immediate first impression: "In this highly colorful crowd, I'm white only." Somehow, I felt deprived.

Since then, I have experienced that same feeling a thousand times in manifold forms: on the subway in Chicago's South Side during the tense summers of the 1960s, as the only white person and the focus of all eyes; in Mexico—nothing in our European sensibility can compare to the pride and the smiling complicity of the person who asserts: *Somos mestizos* (We are mestizos), and *Como Mexico no hay dos* (No other country is like Mexico).

The feeling came back during the years I worked with Virgil Elizondo and the Mexican American Cultural Center he founded. I owe him, and others, the discovery of difference and more importantly, the need to shift my focus beyond Europe.[1]

In the 1960s, it was easy to travel the world with a French passport—at least so I thought at first. Practically all doors opened, and university rituals gave visiting professors the impression they were bringing some of their country's overabundance to what we still then called the third world. It was a wonderful illusion and easily made one its victim. I'm beholden to the people I dealt with for having shown me a new and different road. One day in Lima, someone said, "We aren't asking you to become a Peruvian; simply that, as a Frenchman, you accept a dialogue." In other words, speak together as equals, drop the self-conceit that for five centuries has marked relations between Europe and the other continents, and agree to enter into a process that I perceived as going far beyond intellectual considerations. At first, I didn't try to name this process. I used the usual expressions: international, cultural, or intercultural, and the many derivatives of words being invented at the time.

In this case, too, reality went faster than words. The encounters and the intermixing happening in Latin America and in the New World, happened in Europe, too. In the Lorraine region in the east of France, I was astounded to find a region and a population acutely aware of their identity. Even though half of the inhabitants were not born there, after a few years, they become "Lorraines" and readily proclaimed it.

The wars in Europe left their traces on the Lorraine region. Not just the wars, but the large population shifts too. During the twentieth century, immigrants from Poland, Italy, and North Africa came to work here. A large number of displaced persons arrived after World War II. Dozens of languages are spoken here and, in one way or another, every member of a Lorraine family is bilingual.

I felt like I was back in Texas: an area of borders, which people ceaselessly cross and where cultures commingle and confront each other. Was this "intercultural"? The world had materialized and was spreading, no longer referring to what was far away, but designating the here and now, involving everyday life. It nibbled at previously clearcut linguistic areas. "Intercultural" was precisely a way of designating what did not fit into pre-established categories. Love and gastronomy, the way we celebrate or mourn: ordinary life is henceforward multicultural.

At the same time as *cultural* or *multicultural*, the word *mestizo* insinuated itself into the most unexpected contexts: mestizo encounters, mestizo cultures, music, newspapers. What to do with a word that applies to a world far away, yet a word found at the borders of Europe and even in the heart of our cities? The word's presence in itself indicated the new reality of our societies.

We have some difficulty naming this reality. Looking squarely at it proves even more difficult. It is true that every encounter has two sides. Delight, but also violence. Delight over discovering the other person, this unknown entity; violence because of fear and because one's own identity is threatened. Therein lies the ambivalence in the word *mestizo*. This word elicits both fascination and apprehension, attraction and rejection. It is deeply rooted in the dark zones of our instinct. It has to do with sexuality and the body. Originally associated with the notion of race, *mestizo* is a word invested with the same ambivalence and anathema. *Race, racism:* two words with a potential charge of aggressiveness and violence. Can the word *mestizo* exorcize this violence? By opening up these forbidden zones, can *mestizo* contribute to the possibility of looking at them dispassionately, benevolently, finding in them a new direction for humanity?

Looking honestly at *Mestizaje* is a way for Europe to begin a vast change in mentality: admitting the end of its political—even more, its intellectual and cultural—hegemony. "*Mestizaje*": a positive way for Europe to express the transformation of identities and human relations taking place on its soil. Actually this is no different from what has always happened in Europe, but strangely enough, the last centuries have not wanted to recognize it. Europe is a mestizo continent. We are beginning to hear this. Europe is indubitably a continent of intermix-ings. France in particular was built upon a constant influx and com-mingling of people with different origins. So, why hide this fact, or try to forget it?

Myself and the other person, the one and the many, origin and identity: how do these concepts and notions continue shaping the peoples of Europe? Can *Mestizaje* serve them as a paradigm for their precedent adventure or allow them to exorcize the insane dreams of the twentieth century which brought them such sorrow? If de Gaulle's aphorism has any truth, what meaning do we make of it, how do we live up to it? The goal of this book is to shed some light on possible answers.[2]

We begin by looking at what is meant by *multicultural* and how we name what is at stake in an attempt to discern its possibilities and its limits. Then we'll attempt to give content to the word *Mestizaje* by looking at its place in history and the way thinking about it has evolved. This approach will enable us to determine its symbolic charge as well as ascertain what type of future it opens up.

Notes

1. Cf. Virgil ELIZONDO, *L'avenir est au metissage*, Paris, Mame-Editions Universitaires, 1987. Preface by Léopold Sédar SENGHOR.

2. There exist books on the history of *mestizaje* as well as literary texts, narratives, and novels, but very few texts on *mestizaje* per se. Cf. Francois LAPLANTINE, Alexis NOUSS, *Le Métissage*, Paris, Flammarion, coll. Dominos, 1997. According to the authors: "If, to our best knowledge, no book on *Mestizaje* per se exists, the reason is probably because it's a highly diversified phenomenon and one in perpetual evolution" (pg. 10).

CHAPTER ONE

~

Diversity, Geography, Cultures

The entire world is in my street, in my city, and every big city. Keep eyes and ears open: African *boubous*, North African *djellabas*, Asian faces, musical accents. In the space of a few seconds people pass by whose gait, physical features, skin color, language, gestures, and behavior display a wide variety. As in a kaleidoscope, forms and colors are constantly transformed. Thanks to the present minglings and mergings, humanity has never been in a better position to fully recognize its extreme diversity. We instinctively search for indications. We primarily use geographical reference points when we try to situate people somewhere on the face of the earth.

In the Beginning Was Geography

In the past our schoolbooks explained, without omitting the appropriate illustrations, that our planet was inhabited by four major "races": white, black, yellow, and red. Each race had its continent. Europe was white; Africa, black; Asia, yellow; America, red. In this way, the earth was charted, and everyone clearly, neatly situated. Montesquieu in the eighteenth century, for example, agreed with the ancient Greeks and maintained that geographical differences—climate and terrain—could account for the differences in behavior and laws among human societies. He explained "how men differ significantly according to their different climates" or likewise, that the domination of weak peoples by strong ones could be traced to the differences between hot and cold climates.[1] These classifications of traditional geography continue functioning spontaneously in our minds. They motivate our immediate reactions and underpin the clichés heard at the local café, even though we know things are not so simple, even if our geography books today are more nuanced and approach human diversity from angles other than skin color.

These classifications invoke angles like habitat and behavior—a geography of customs, traditions, ways of living. If we can differentiate a Japanese from an African, a German from a Mexican, it's because of clothing, cuisine, the way he or she organizes time, language, and not merely because of physical characteristics. In other words, countries are not just a geographical place, physically delimited by oceans, mountains, rivers. They are territories that have been occupied for millennia by groups of human beings having modeled these spaces and been modeled by them according to conditions found there. The customs and traditions of the Inuits, or sub-Saharan Africans, or people of the Himalayas, or the Mediterranean peoples, or Northern Europeans were invented in order to survive. Each of these groups had to imagine how to best adjust to their environment, how to protect themselves from it and how to use its resources. To speak of these groups is to speak of a geographical territory and also the manner of surviving and thriving there elaborated over centuries: in short, to speak of *cultures*. Geographical diversity and cultural variety go hand in hand. Trying to establish some reference points amid the continuous flow of human diversity requires considering the geographical aspect of territory as well as the social aspect of culture.

It's impossible for individuals to take no account of the land on which they were born, no account of their ancestors' territory. In a thousand ways, the body carries the marks of these roots and their soil, marks going way beyond physique, skin color, or facial features. A territory means landscapes, a specific soil and particular living conditions. Behind each face can be guessed a distinctive horizon. It's quite different to be born on the edge of the Indian Ocean or on the High Plateau of South America, near a river in a gentle, sunny valley or on water-starved land. This memory inscribed in our bodies, beyond our conscious perceptions, is simultaneously a limit and our precious treasure. There is no sense in trying to divest ourselves of it; no matter what, it remains. Human beings are "sons and daughters of the earth." Their bodies are eloquent. This rootedness in one's body confers on human beings a sort of "kinship" with indigenous plants and animals. It makes each person a unique being, not interchangeable with others; individuals and groups are dependent on their location. The social bond includes a geographical dimension. The word *race* in its broad sense described this geographical diversity of identities. Identities varied according to geography. *Mestizaje* was first used to describe the encounter of bodies despite distance. The dictionary definition is: the mixing of races. The mestizo child is born of parents coming from separate geographic zones. He/She makes us aware that the reality of human relations is rooted in the body.

However, territorial reference points go hand in hand with cultural ones. It's true that each country corresponds to a territory, but each country is home to one or several groups whose characteristics are not determined by geography alone. In fact, in our search for clues, we increasingly make mistakes. We are obliged to be hesitant. Although individuals are marked by their own geographical origins and by the place their ancestors came from, it's no longer possible to unfailingly link geography and appearance. Geography is quickly revealed to be insufficient. And yesterday's categories are increasingly inadequate for situating individuals. Reality has rendered appearance obsolete as a means of classifying people, as we spontaneously used to do.

We are unable to situate many of the people we observe around us. The usual clues used to determine origins—exterior appearance, clothing, language, behavior—are inoperative, the usual categories too simplistic. Maybe if we try hard, someone's appearance might evoke a territory. They themselves, or their ancestors, were born elsewhere, but that place is no longer home. Maybe a little something is left, an accent or certain gestures, but they left these foreign lands a long time ago. Now they are citizens of the planet's metropolises. They are part of the population shifts occurring even in the furthest reaches of our globe.

In the remotest village in France or in Africa we can meet—what a surprise!—men and women from far-off lands whose stories tell anew of humanity's age-old, ongoing itinerancy. So that it is not geography that permits situating these human beings; it is their story, the road traveled by them and their ancestors: not in terms of the physical territory spanned, as with plants and animals, but in terms of time, which gives its constancy to the human adventure.

The World Cup in 1998 was a remarkable illustration. Obviously each team was defined first of all by country. The players sported the national colors, and their fans rallied around the nation's flag. France, Brazil, Croatia, Cameroon. But on closer look, a story was embedded in each player going far beyond his passport. He was born here, yet behind him could be glimpsed a line of ancestors born in foreign countries. From this point of view, the French team was exemplary. Basque, Breton, Kabyle, Kanak, Parisian, or Caribbean, the players formed one team, from one country. "Multicolored France," "Mestizo France," said the headlines. The newspaper *Le Monde* wrote: "It's possible to be the son or the grandson of Africans, to have roots in the Antilles or in New Caledonia and yet incarnate the nation to the point of becoming a national hero."[2]

Even if it's impossible to forget geography and origins, it's also impossible to be satisfied with them as a reference point in the mobility of our cities. We need to move past old categories and the simplistic, schoolbook classifications dividing the "races" into four: white, black, yellow, and red! We need to find other means of classifying human diversity. Geographical diversity points to cultural variety.

Cultural Indicators

What an impressive list of words and expressions has appeared over the last few years to designate what is happening before our very eyes. *Cultural, intercultural, multicultural, the blending or the confrontation of cultures, pluralism, cultural plurality, multiculturalism* . . . and no doubt the list will continue to grow. All these words and expressions derive more or less from the word *culture*. Their unprecedented appearance in daily conversations indicates that something is taking place in our societies and highlights our willingness to find a new and original way of naming it. Let us take a look at the root word, *culture*. Its sudden and widespread use indicates that it represents a particular way of comprehending reality. Originally a technical word, it's now part of ordinary vocabulary. It proposes a new grasp of experience. Taking a good look at this word makes it possible to capture the scope of words composed from it and which continue coming forth every day.

Culture is a word of many meanings. Depending on who uses it and when, its signification varies. It has different meanings in different languages, and translations sometimes have difficulty in rendering its nuances. But more so than its dictionary meaning, what provokes the most varied attitudes and emotions—fascination or rejection, attraction or fear—are its connotations.

To begin at the beginning, *culture*, in the European languages stemming from Latin, has at least two quasi-universally present significations. Its first, and for a long time sole, meaning is: "That which is related to the development of the mind." In broader terms, the word *culture* evokes civilization, the image that a people forge of themselves, the progress they have made through education, science, or the arts. In short, the place accorded by a people to reason and intellectual accomplishments. Europeans consider themselves highly cultivated people, not without a touch of condescension toward individuals or groups they consider "uncivilized" or "uncultivated." This classic meaning of *culture* implies a value judgment.

Culture in its more recent meaning designates the whole of any given group's way of living, from their representations of the world, to their tools, rites, and customs. According to this meaning, all peoples possess a culture, and it becomes impossible to say that some are cultivated while others are not. *Culture* indicates what is specifically human, what sets humans apart from other animals and makes them more than just a "natural" being.

To be truthful, the idea that humans have some kind of natural state, unaffected by nurture, is just a notion. What distinguishes humans from animals is precisely the fact that humans possess a culture and the other species don't, even the ones we consider as being closest to us. Human beings make tools and constantly improve them. They speak not just an exchange of signs and sounds, but an organized language. Humans create multiple languages and constantly update and modify them. It's not enough to say that a human is a social animal. Many other species have also developed societies. But what makes human beings human is that they are beings possessing a culture. "Among living beings, man alone uses devices like speech and tools in his dealings with other people and with his environment.[3]

In this case *culture* designates what makes each group unique and how they are actors in the human adventure using their own language, customs, tools, lifestyle. This definition holds equally true for every group. Used this way, the word *culture* implies no discrimination. It assigns equal value to every person. This ethnological meaning is the one that predominated during the twentieth century, especially in the Anglo-Saxon world, because of the influence of the human sciences.

This is the meaning used in this book. It represents a shift in the point of view on reality. It enables comprehending the other—individual or society—in what intimately constitutes his/her identity, beyond particular traits and labels. It allows getting a grasp on an individual's or a group's ongoing existence, precisely before all analysis and its resultant limiting definitions. The paradoxical result is that evoking culture gives simultaneous access to what is most specific and most universal in an individual or a group. The noun *culture* and the adjective *cultural* are like "jokers" in daily conversations, introducing an element of surprise and auguring important winnings.

In our present situation of population mixes, the word *culture* and its derivatives hold out hope for the possibility of determining the exact roots of our divisions and oppositions: "They are of different cultures!" These words also hold out the hope of a reconciliation. "The future belongs to interculturalism" becomes a key affirmation in many situations. If we want less imprecision, we must face the rigors of a few clarifying remarks, since *culture* has different connotations depending on the situations in which it is used.

The word *culture* is a relatively recent addition to everyday vocabulary, at least with the meaning we give it. At the end of the nineteenth century, the Grand Larousse dictionary uses it in the sense of agriculture and concedes a derived meaning: a cultivated person—the classic meaning mentioned earlier. The word begins gradually to have another meaning. Ethnologists begin to use it instead of *race*. For specialists, the word gained acceptance thanks to Anglo Saxon anthropology, illustrated by the prestigious names of Edward Tylor, Bronislaw Malinowski, Ruth Benedict, and Margaret Mead. The American School of Anthropology particularly stressed the diversity of cultures, the specificity of each human group, and the coherence of the material and symbolic elements composing its existence.

Thanks to the work of scientists, *culture* gains a precise meaning. It no longer refers to the universal man of classic humanism: that ideal personality who could be considered a "cultured person" thanks to a good upbringing and well-rounded knowledge. On the contrary, the word designates the things ethnology focuses on, that is, human diversity, the multitude of experiences, outlooks, lifestyles, and the uniqueness of each people due to their specific modes of existence, representations of the world and values. Anthropology puts an end to the illusion that all human groups are similar, with the white man having the normative role. Other traditions, other human groups, other cultures exist in their own right, neither minor, nor deserving of scorn, nor outdated. Sharing in the human adventure can be done in multiple ways, all equally deserving of respect. Humanity is a rainbow of situations and traditions, as varied as the rainbow of colors. The word *culture* becomes a heuristic tool, helping us to recognize and give value to human diversity.

For the general public, *culture* took on its modern signification with the Bandung (Indonesia) Conference from April 18–24, 1955. A fascinating and almost subversive aura surrounded it. Twenty-nine third world countries, including India and China, proclaimed their rejection of all forms of colonialism and affirmed their desire for political liberation and economic independence. These countries affirmed a role for themselves not aligned with either of the two blocks: the capitalist West or the Marxist Soviet Union. One of the key words of this affirmation was *culture*. It referred to a singular identity and proclaimed the *right to be different* for peoples whose wealth could not be assessed in terms of money and the stock exchange, but lay in their accumulated history and traditions. Ten years after the conference, China underwent its *cultural revolution*, with its cortege of destruction and death, which profoundly shook and troubled the country.

After Bandung, *culture* becomes a powerful word, charged with political violence. All over the planet, this word becomes an instrument used by the poor countries in their struggle against the rich countries. It heralds the worldwide appearance of new forces. The rich and powerful countries are no longer the only ones deciding the rules of the game. Political minorities, and soon all minorities, claim the right to decide them too. One's singularity, both ethnic and symbolic, is transformed into an instrument of action. The word *culture* is endowed with political value, becoming a weapon in the conflict between groups.

This combat didn't take long to reach the developed countries. The new awareness and the challenges to established order caused by the third world penetrated the whole of society. In our countries, the word *culture* became a subject of debate when, during 1968, from Santiago, Chile, to Mexico City and Paris, students demonstrated in the name of the *cultural revolution*, sometimes paying a heavy price for challenging the established order. The student movements, sometimes lightheartedly, sometimes tragically, made governments everywhere tremble, causing the departure of de Gaulle in France and a bloody repression in Mexico.

This tidal wave challenged the very underpinnings of developed societies. More than a mere modification of society's collective behavior was called for, and traditional mechanisms of parliamentary democracies were insufficient to resolve the crisis. What was required had to do with redefining the identity of each peoples and the ways human beings could live together side by side. The issues and challenges set in motion in the third world continued their incursions in the developed countries, and especially to the universities, the centers of thought and discussion where the future is being prepared. At the same time that these questions were being debated, there were large migrations of people and these inevitably challenged the organization of riches and the exercise of power. They pointed to the ultimate questions: "Who am I?," "Who are we?," and "How do we live together?" Racial questions like these strike precisely at the foundations of the human adventure. *Culture* thereby acquires an existential significance. It evokes a two-pronged experience: the experience of each group's uniqueness and the experience of the diversity of identities.

Culture and the derived adjective *cultural* had achieved their place in the sun, with a triple signification: ethnological, political, and descriptive of identity. These words signified what allows a group of humans to survive, the whole set of material and symbolic elements that forge an identity. This definition applied equally to all peoples, whether economically underdeveloped or advanced. In a few years, this word, formerly used mainly by scholars, had become a key word for understanding oneself and the world; it was particularly suited to expressing identity and diversity.

Culture is a word that throws into relief what is at stake in our actions. In the beginning, this apparently inoffensive word simply indicated that attention was being paid to the other person's difference. However, in contemplating the other person, we contemplate ourselves and are forced to recognize the positives and the negatives we have within us. Taking culture into account invites dialogue but also reveals the difficulties of dialogue. Speaking of *culture* in reference to someone else is both a way of recognizing the specificity of each identity and a way of stressing the differences. Everyone has a culture, and no two cultures are alike. Yet it is also a way of affirming that something is shared by all humans. Everyone possesses a culture. The contrary would make humanity impossible. Acknowledging each person with their specific culture means acknowledging them as human.

Therein lies the paradox: acknowledging a person in their specific culture, thereby accenting their difference, is at the same time acknowledging them as human and accenting their similarity to me. This give and take between differences and resemblance is fraught with potential violence. Our shared humanity encourages encounters and fellowship. Differences have in them a potential for conflicts named *exclusion, discrimination, racism.* By using the word *culture*, we call for a change in our outlook, in our attitudes, and in the ways we live. The encounter of cultures is not to be taken for granted. It does not resemble a genteel conversation. Relations between people are not simple nor are they easily ordered and organized. Every encounter represents a flesh and blood commitment, leaving questions of organization and polity in the dust. Every encounter initiates a high-risk trajectory between confinement and exchange, destruction and survival. The word *culture* is thus charged with the dense weight of humanity.

In recent years, several words stemming from *culture* help us to get a better focus on this paradox. These words simultaneously speak of encounter and risk. Consider a few of the many derivatives whose meanings evolve or are similar. *Intercultural* designates an exchange between two or more cultures. Travels abroad and seminars are referred to as intercultural experiences. *Pluricultural* refers to the juxtaposition of different cultural rootings in any given society. *Multicultural* puts the accent on the variety of feelings generated by these different cultural origins and how these assorted experiences interact. We define our societies as pluricultural or multicultural. Trying to ascertain what multiculturalism means is part of society's ongoing debate.

Culture and Modernity

In fact, the classic meaning of *culture* and its meaning in human sciences coexist and permeate each other. The classic meaning also connotes modernity, that is, the superiority of reason over the obscure forces of dream or myth, while the meaning given by the human sciences, especially ethnology, seems to reinstate what science had for a time definitively discarded: the importance of the customs, rites, and beliefs specific to any given group of people. The first meaning implies a break with the past, while the second one seems to validate a re-emergence or the permanence of age-old energies. We can speak of intercultural only within the second meaning, since according to the first meaning, culture, being a product of intellect and reason, is considered unique and, in theory, universal, since groups can evolve to it.

Reason and dreams, present and past, universal and particular—*culture* can evoke both, depending on context. As a result, speaking about what is intercultural has less to do with comparing culture X and culture Y, than with questioning each culture's relation to modernity. It is a culture's relation to modernity that allows comparing cultures. Culture X's relation to Culture Y depends on X and Y's individual relation to modernity. What we name modernity, to be succinct, habitually designates the change in civilization that began with the eighteenth century Enlightenment and that transformed ways of thinking and living in European societies. This movement represented a break with the past because it was a vehicle for the new forms of knowledge and action represented by science and technology. This movement also affirmed a new existential principle: the autonomy of human reason, postulating that the individual was governed by reason, and society by democracy.

This situation divides societies into those preceding and those following modernity. In those preceding modernity, identity is determined by an individual's ethnic group, customs and traditions, and family and bloodlines, and this is what is generally meant by the word *race*. Identity means first of all being designated as *the son/daughter of* this father, this family, this tribe, this people. Societies proceeding from modernity are defined by reason and law. Through the development of science and technology, these societies want to promote the advent of universal man, whose new identity is expressed in the idea of human rights. This new identity is rooted in the social contract, the acceptance of jointly established laws, rooted in civic ties. In this type of society, identity means considering oneself a citizen of a nation, accepting the responsibilities and benefiting from the rights conferred with this status.

Culture, intercultural, or *multicultural* have different meanings depending on whether or not we're talking about societies that embrace modernity or ones that reject it. Need we be reminded that things are never so simple or clear-cut in reality? Today, no society on the face of the Earth can avoid coming into contact with various manifestations of modernity, and all societies oscillate between tradition and modernity. On one side there are ethnic links, customs, and ancient stories, myths, religion, deep emotions yoked to the body. On the other, there are the democratic bond, the national and the international, the law, but also innovation, rationality, science, and progress.

Perhaps we believed too readily that pre and postmodernity followed each other on a straight line and that it was easy to go from one to the other, with the second almost automatically voiding the first. Bandung, and especially the cultural revolutions of the 1960s, epitomized that the revolt of different peoples is somewhere between these two poles, and we are searching for valid models of how to link the two. Human beings are obliged to partake of both poles, even in the most optimistic of utopias. What is determinant are the forms taken by the relationship between these two aspects of human identity.

Consequently, *multicultural* does not designate some hazardous mix or some distant magical point where simply evoking culture resolves all problems, legitimates all differences, erases conflicts, and acknowledges the plurality of identities, or a point where the son and the citizen seamlessly coincide, where the memory of a native soil harmoniously meshes with history rather than confronting history as it presently does. *Multicultural* designates an attempt to articulate between various, clearly situated elements, with modernity playing the discerning role indicated above. Given the diversity of situations, trajectories, and frictions within and among human groups, this articulation is a way of bringing to light the possibilities offered for promoting coexistence and profiting from our differences.

But the line to cross is called modernity. We can speak of the meeting of cultures only after crossing this line. This is why the subject of what multiculturalism is and what it signifies is an urgent question in the countries already well into modernity, first and foremost in the developed, western world. The concept of multiculturalism doesn't have the same ramifications if we are dealing with so-called "primitive" societies whose survival depends on a certain isolation, or on urbanized, developed societies. Claude Lévi-Strauss, referring to his experience with the Amerindians, warns against too much cultural mixing. The difference between groups is of course a prerequisite for encounter, yet this difference is endangered by the encounter. Lévi-Strauss states:

> When all is said and done, it's difficult to consider as anything but contradictory a process that can be summarized in the following manner: in order to progress, humans must cooperate; and in the course of their cooperation they witness their specific contributions gradually becoming identical, these very contributions whose initial diversity was precisely what made their cooperation fertile and necessary.[4]

We are talking here about "primitive" cultures, which risk destruction through too-rapid exposure to modern cultures. That is why Lévi-Strauss insists that a necessary condition for a culture's survival is that it have sufficient geographical territory. However, it's a completely different situation from the Amazon forest when we consider our large cities where Lévi-Strauss's contradiction is confronted daily. What renders the satiation novel is precisely the fact that people of extremely varied geographical and cultural origins are obliged, rapidly and without the slightest transition, to coexist in the restricted space of urban life. The rapid shifting of populations and their massive arrival in the big cities create a new situation, and this situation is the subject of all the thought and reflection going on around the concept of multiculturalism.

People who are born in North Africa or Mali find themselves living in Paris with no transition of any kind. In the next street over or across the hall, they meet Vietnamese, or people from the Antilles or Canada.

At school, their children are in contact with people of twenty different origins. In the marketplace, they can choose between European products, products from the Indian Ocean, or those from the Antilles. The simple words of daily existence are pronounced in a multitude of accents, and words from different foreign languages, designating clothing, food, religion, slowly seep into the language of their new country.

This is the situation for which we habitually use the word *multiculturalism*. The prefix *multi* evokes not only the variety and the plurality of origins and attachments but also the mix, profusion, mobility, and diversity created by this variety. In an attempt to offer a few reference points in this incessant movement, careful thought about multiculturalism is needed.

Geographical reference points clearly no longer suffice. Geography was formerly a way of classifying diversity. One nation, one culture. And for a long time, the European nations lived under the illusion that this was true for them too. History, however, reminds them that the homogeneity they claim for themselves was not something innate but acquired over time and with violence. Today it's impossible to claim this homogeneity as natural and normal. Many cultures are now present on any given territory. This constantly growing diversity has a favorite place: the city.

Reference points linked to the past also no longer suffice. Neither can ancestral origins help us to classify people. People here have left their native countries and, whatever nostalgia they may have, their life is now defined by the future, a future to be built and shared with others living in the same territory.

We are forced to pay attention to what's going on here and now, to the mingling of human beings, so different and yet so alike, people of multiple origins who live on the same land and thus are forced to shape a common existence. These groups are not inert, they constantly and colorfully interact, mixing sounds and colors, traditions and lifestyles. Through marriage this mixing produces mestizo children. This word has acquired a new meaning in daily conversations. Why mestizos? Because they are a mix of different ethnic groups, or of different races, if we use the old terminology. But they are mestizo too because they are a mix of different cultures, countries, or nations. The meanings this word encompasses are expanding. An alternative exists to the fears expressed by

Lévi-Strauss. Differences don't disappear. They are transformed. They give birth to new differences, and the word *mestizaje* accents these new differences. A humanity of widespread *mestizaje* is in no danger of monotony. There is increasing talk of *cultural mestizaje*. After considering the implications of *multicultural*, we must now explore *mestizaje* in order to interpret and explain the human diversity at work in our cities.

Notes

1. Cf. *De l'Esprit des Lois*, Part 3, Book XIV to XVIII.
2. *Le Monde*, July 24, 1998.
3. Cf. Michel LEIRIS, *Cinq études d'éthnologie*, Paris, Denoël, 1969.
4. Claude LÉVI-STRAUSS, *Anthropologie structurale deux*, Paris, Plon, 1973, pg. 420:

Quoi qu'il en soit, il est difficite de se représenter autrement que comme contradictoire, un processus que l'on peut résumer de la façon suivante: pour grogesser, il faut que les hommes collaborent ; et au cours de leur collaboration, ils viient gradueliement s'identifier les apports dont la diversité initiale était précisément ce qui rendait leur collaboration féconde et nécessaire.

~

CHAPTER TWO

From Multicultural
to *Mestizaje*

As I watch passersby, I can follow each one, at least in my imagination. Where are they coming from? Going to? What they do is familiar: shop, take the subway, drive the kids to school. But to what do these actions correspond? In what existences are they rooted? What projects do these people have? Tonight they will return to a family or at least to a home and neighbors. They dream about a vacation in the old country, work to insure the future of their children, speak of their plans to make the pilgrimage to Mecca or refurbish that house in Portugal. The actions are the same but behind them are various private worlds. Every man, every woman carries a different world within.

The contact between these worlds seems to be smooth, flowing to the tempo of the crowd going by. From time to time there is a spark, voices become louder, insults erupt in different languages. And then the flow calmly resumes. But maybe not, for subtle barriers divide the neighborhood. That street is Pakistani territory, further up, it's the Turkish restaurant, here the neighbors circulated a petition against the African store because there was too much noise at night, with people congregating in the middle of the street. Daily coexistence can have its surprises. Categories easily get put on people. Stereotypes are prompt to resurface and conflicts get nasty. The biggest conflicts wind up in court perhaps over a leak in the pipes or a late payment. Indeed, how does one make people understand that an apartment in Paris is not the same thing as a house in a small village below the equator, or that *creditor* is not a synonym for *lender?*

The crowd flows by, but everyone is on their guard, and behind the reassuring facade of similar actions, latent violence is always present. Daily-life multiculturalism is no sinecure. Every person is unlike the next, and knows it. Everyone is aware that the other considers him different, and in a certain way, considers him guilty of being different. Each person knows a word or a gesture might be all it takes for aggressive attitudes to erupt, knows that we are all "strangers" here and therefore feel threatened.

Once we are aware of this, what we need to do is go beyond a superficial reaction to these differences and find a way to make living together possible for populations foreign to one another. We need to find an answer to the question "What kind of community can we create and perpetuate from the diverse human beings we are?" as Amy Gutmann says.[1] We need to identify what furthers this coexistence and offers models of coexistence between people of different cultures that allow individuals to forge their identities and afford them recognition. How can we promote the coexistence in close proximity of individuals or groups with differing origins, traditions, and cultures? In a way, coexistence is too weak a word, because what we're talking about is ensuring everyone not just equal political rights but also a social and cultural environment providing them a dignified existence; "A cultural context bestowing significance and perspective to the choices they have made for their lives."[2] This is what multiculturalism is all about.

Recognizing Differences

Multiculturalism is a recent word. Stemming from the American tradition, it took hold in the 1980s, in the course of debates over equality between different groups in the United States and over the "politically correct" attitude toward minorities. In his book, *Multiculturalism and the Politics of Recognition*, published in 1992, Charles Taylor contributed significantly to this debate by proposing a philosophical grounding for it. A professor in Montreal, one of the most cosmopolitan cities in the West, Taylor naturally wrote with his city's case in mind, but also the situation of Quebec and of the English-speaking provinces.

Recognition is the key category used by Taylor in elaborating possible societal models. Recognition "designates something like a person's understanding of who they are, of their fundamental defining characteristics as a human being."[3] Our identity as individuals or groups depends on whether or not we are acknowledged and appreciated.

In other words, cultural diversity has as a corollary: how individuals perceive themselves and others, and the acceptance—the recognition—of this perception enables an individual's self-definition and self-expression. The sequence is: variety of cultures, perception of the differences stemming from this variety, identity. The collective and the subjective aspects of culture are thus articulated. Recognition is the pivot point of this articulation. The human diversity we talk about in the preceding chapter cannot be isolated from the way individuals perceive it. It cannot be separated from the way they experience it, how they define themselves and how they are defined by others.

Taylor traces the historical evolution of the concept of recognition in the West. He points out that in ancient societies, recognition is linked to hierarchy; individuals are identified and accepted according to the place and the role they occupy in a given hierarchical order. Being recognized is a factor of the honor due to each person because of his or her rank. Although not actually fostering it himself, Jean-Jacques Rousseau pointed the way to a decisive reversal. With Rousseau, identity is no longer a function of an individual's role in society. It doesn't depend on his or her position in a hierarchy. Henceforward, what defines individuals is their inner authenticity. The age of honor is followed by the age of dignity, and the consequence is "a politics of universalism emphasizing the equal dignity of all citizens."[4]

This is where the difficulty comes in; to what does the belief in universal dignity lead? It leads to respect. Respect for universal reason which characterizes humanity and represents a primordial element of dignity. Respect for differences, too. Acknowledging differences, whether between individuals or groups, means paying attention to them, respecting them, simply because they are specific aspects of a shared identity as humans.

The movement that links cultural diversity to individual subjectivity has two strands. One strand values and respects each culture precisely because of its particularities, its differences. And at the same time, the

other strand values what makes each culture a part of something universal as well as its aspirations to this universality. At the very heart of this
concept of recognition we find the conflict between the universal and
the particular. It's no longer possible to consider resolving this conflict by
some predetermined social hierarchy or by some national or ideological
order assigning a predetermined rank to every individual, group, or culture. A supposedly superior order, universally recognized, no longer exists. Consequently, in the context of a common humanity, no one can
claim that one culture is superior to another. This is the paradox of recognition: even as it asserts its attention to the particular, it affirms the universal.

A tension therefore arises between the politics of equal dignity and
the politics of difference. Theoretically, the two imperatives mesh. But
their practical application leads to potentially contradictory concrete
demands.

> With the politics of equal dignity, what is established is meant to be uni-
> versally the same, an identical basket of rights and immunities; with the
> politics of difference, what we are asked to recognize is the unique iden-
> tity of this individual or group, their distinctness from everyone else.[5]

These are the two faces of recognition according to Taylor, and
they cannot be dissociated. Ignoring either one, or merging them,
leads to justifying domination and betraying the ideal of authenticity. Multiculturalism's biggest challenge is how to articulate the
two. Reconciling the two faces is far from automatic because each
culture is specific and specially defined and every culture has the
right to be placed on an equal footing with the others. But a "neutral" and "exterior" viewpoint that could order differences and
avoid friction doesn't exist. Multiculturalism is predicated on the
possibility of having both equality *and* difference in equal measure and elaborating a multicultural society. At this point Taylor
exercises prudence:

> There must be something midway between the inauthentic and homog-
> enizing demand for recognition of equal worth on the one hand, and
> self-aggrandizing within ethnocentric standards, on the other. There are

other cultures, and we have to live together more and more, both on a world scale and commingled in each individual society.[6]

In practice, Taylor opens the door to several strands of multicultur-alism, which Michaël Walzer systematizes.[7] We can imagine a society that welcomes cultural diversity as reflected by the diversity of individuals, with the intention of incorporating them slowly into a new, common culture. On the other hand, we can imagine a society that makes a place for the diversity of groups, accepting their differing life choices and allowing them to create concrete, collective conditions in order to flourish. In short, there are two major possibilities: either a common, collective framework where differences are relegated to the private sphere, or a common framework within which a group's differences are accepted and given legitimate space.

France finds itself in the first case, where the laws of the Republic, and the social identity they ground, are the same for everyone. Recognition in this example is a case of granting whoever lives on French soil the same rights; differences in treatment are considered inequalities or discriminations. Particularisms, customs, lifestyles are a matter of individual choice and are not a problem unless they clash with the country's laws and commonly accepted rules and regulations. Consider the issue of official language. Everyone can speak the language they wish but schools teach French, the official language of courts and civil administration. Civil service exams are taken in French, and individuals must master this language to hold any public position. In this way, a process of integration continues which—at least we can hope— eventually leads to a certain form of homogeneity for all the people living in a particular land. Every person is "French," and that is precisely what enables individual differences to be cultivated and safeguarded.

The other case according to Taylor is exemplified by Canada, where he was born (Taylor, to be truthful, crafted his theory with his native country in mind.) Recognition implies in this case that a certain number of a group's demands be acknowledged in law. In Quebec, for example, French is used as an official language. In the absence of recognition for certain collective behavior that differs from that of the other groups in the country, the very survival of the group is endangered. This strand of multiculturalism is justified in the name of minority culture survival and of a future for the particularities that identify a culture, in this case, the culture of French-speaking Quebeckers. There is a similar issue concerning the use of the Spanish language in the southwestern United States.

The New World found itself forced to recognize the particularisms of its Indian societies. It is impossible to dissolve them in the "melting pot." More than ever, the Indians are asserting their distinctive identities and demanding from public institutions the collective conditions for their identities to exist and flourish. The most recent example is the creation in April 1999 of Nunavat, the Inuits' autonomous territory. This established that coexistence should be allowed within any given territory of groups whose language, customs, and mores are different. Even some aspects of their legal system may differ, and acknowledging them may be taken to the point of creating special courts for certain types of misdemeanors. Recognition no longer means acknowledging individual singularities; it means recognizing collective particularisms, those of the distinct cultural groups sharing the same territory.

Beyond Multiculturalism

Taylor's ideas show the importance of shattering the illusion of a *melting pot* homogenizing individuals into one unique culture. Taylor welcomes cultural diversity and the wealth it brings and goes on to describe the elements for political and legal management of the situation. The debate is not *a priori* resolved by the strongest group, which, by imposing its language, religion, and customs, denies others the right to survive. Taylor offers liberal societies perspective for the future. Proposing possible paths to coexistence, he suggests breaking out of the following alternative: either violence imposed by a dominant society, or else a headlong escape into the utopian unreality of a large, universal brotherhood.

This is where the debate gets interesting. Taylor's philosophical distinctions are clear and stimulating, but putting the proposed models into practice raises multiple questions. Particularly in France, where the debate on multiculturalism takes place in the context of the recurrent standoff between France and the United States with its attendant fascination *cum* rejection. Is the American brand of multiculturalism a "demon" to be exorcized, or on the contrary, is it a model to be examined profitably? And why not imagine a French brand of multiculturalism?

> The scarecrow of American-style multiculturalism is periodically agitated in France whenever there's a new societal debate. We are purportedly menaced by a future of autistic ethnic communities, no longer having any common values and which would be like so many prisons for their members.[8]

As this observation demonstrates, in actual practice, matters are not so simple. Concrete situations cannot be made to fit smoothly into neat theoretical models. Not in France, nor in the United States.[9] So, his proposition is:

> Maybe it could be possible to some extent to correct the centripetal forces at work in French society by injecting a dose of multiculturalism, while American society, purportedly suffering from a centrifugal tropism, would have something to gain by taking a leaf from our republican tradition.[10]

The debate will not be over soon because it is as much a question of paying close attention to the practicalities of encounters between cultures as it is of refining theoretical concepts. This book's aim is not to prolong this debate but to draw attention, from another vantage point, to the limits of multiculturalism. In effect, the current thinking on multiculturalism scarcely provides any elements that can serve as a basis for discerning how to recognize these limitations. However much there may be agreement about the necessity of such a recognition, there is still a paucity of practical applications. Even Taylor is extremely prudent. He speaks of *something midway* and of *new mixes*. He mentions the difficulty of the undertaking. He insists on its *dialogical* nature, that it is based on an exchange. Scholars who may want to get beyond peremptory schemas seem obliged to be infinitely nuanced in their descriptions of the concrete ways of achieving recognition of multiculturalism's limitations.

There is also a limit that stems from the fact that cultural differences do not remain forever the same. The differences between people—cultural diversity—are at the heart of the recognition process precisely because they are the expression of every individual's own humanity. These differences are what need to be compared, confronted, risked in dialogue, through the give-and-take of concrete interaction between people. This risk includes accepting change. Indeed, recognition sets in motion human intersubjectivity. Dialogue must necessarily be a dialogue between subjects. This implies that I, as well as the other, accede to the status of subject, that is, of human beings. Recognition enables human beings to become even more human. The absence of recognition reduces a human being's status and destroys the humanity of both protagonists.

In acknowledging the other, with their distinct culture, I recognize they are human. At the same time, I affirm myself as human. For both protagonists, the process of recognition now becomes a process of transformation, an experience that opens onto a place beyond violence. In other words, recognition modifies protagonists and also modifies, more or less in the long run, identities and cultures. What's at issue here is a transforming recognition. Using this concept may make it possible to extend Taylor's ideas in the two directions mentioned above: the transformation of culture and the process leading to it.

First of all, cultures are not static. They are not inert items to be organized in charts and graphs. It's one thing to be an ethnographer whose role is observing and understanding, and it's another thing to be a politician or simply a citizen who has to deal with a precise situation. It's true that families of Asian, Caribbean, North African, or French origins, living side by side in a Parisian apartment building and having children who go to the same school and play together on the neighborhood playground, refer to themselves, with a certain pride even, in relation to their country of origin. It's true they are Vietnamese, or from Martinique, or Moroccan or from Brittany, but no longer exactly the way they were a few years ago, before they moved here where they live in close proximity. From the minute they enter school for the first time, their children embark upon a process that will change them. Paying attention to clothes, attitudes, conversations is a sufficient illustration of this.

These people are from different places and contexts. They are the leading protagonists of a new and evolving situation, a situation we lack the words to describe. The word *multicultural* and its associated words are insufficient, because they are turned toward origins when it's the future that needs to be addressed. These words sketch the current status of the cultural groups but cannot name the dynamics modifying them. They leave largely unaddressed the relational aspect to recognition, the transforming recognition evoked above. In short, they put a label on the situation, thereby freezing it, by designating what is by what was. What is unprecedented in the situation consequently risks escaping us.

Language tends to congeal things. Of course we know our neighbor is of a different color, celebrates other religious holidays, speaks a mother tongue we don't understand. Of course, we can put his culture in a slot on an imaginary table of cultures. And we can put a reassuring or a troubling label on him, but labels attached to an individual or a group quickly become hateful because they rigidify, congeal, judge, and even kill. Such is the ordinary racism of language, designating some as lazy, others as thieves or self-serving according to their ethnic origins. From the moment that two groups are present on the same territory, they cannot avoid interacting and commingling. Because it's convenient to do so, we continue referring to them by their origins. But they are already no longer what they were, simply because they've crossed a border. Thanks to language, lifestyles, work, and marriages, a "new mix" is born, as Taylor would say.

Such a new mix is not exempt from violence. This is the second aspect we need to highlight in the concept of a transforming recognition, an aspect that the thinking on multiculturalism risks leaving in the shadows. This aspect bears upon the ways people and groups relate. These relations can, of course, be thought of as something relatively easy, as if each culture were somehow aseptic. The word *intercultural* risks leading us into making this assumption and suggests that encounters are amiable events where exchange is easy. And, of course, this can be the case, but often it's a totally different experience, because differences give rise to violence—unexpected violence, violence suffered because of incomprehension or tense, difficult relations. In the present day, relations between groups have been marked by the rule of the strong over the weak. This domination may take the form of war, or brutal enslavement, or the forms of commonplace violence: discrimination and racism. The space of our cities is not the extended geographical space Lévi-Strauss demanded but the space of daily, constant proximity. Proximity exacerbates aggressiveness, and in this kind of context, recognition rapidly runs up against its limits.

Imposing frontiers within the city—not geographical frontiers but legal ones that confine each group and each culture within their own community—doesn't prevent violence. In this case, recognition is neither broad and all-encompassing nor limited to individuals, but it becomes a specific recognition of the customs and traditions of a given group, with its attendant risk of new apartheids. Apartheids are untenable because people do not remain the same and unrealistic since in their desire to avoid violence, they exacerbate it. It is thus impossible to pretend violence doesn't exist or to ignore its risk. We are far from the humanist's view of mankind and the dialogue of cultures! Particularisms glare at each other and take rigid stances. Containing this violence through law is still the first recourse, but the risk is that the result will also be a violence set in cement. Once it's inscribed in law, recognition of particularisms leads to a cultural mosaic that encloses each individual in their group, and this is the opposite of what was originally intended by the idea of a group's accession to modernity.

In other words, whatever the forms of coexistence, multiculturalism invites us to go beyond violence. Dialogue, whatever the inherent difficulties, invites going beyond barriers and meeting as subjects, as people sharing the same territory and, whether they like it or not, partnership in the same adventure. This is when recognition comes into its full significance. It is definitely not a matter of filling in an ethnographer's chart of cultural diversity. What we're talking about is an exchange between human beings. Recognition is its necessary condition; it indicates the direction and requires reciprocity, since this exchange involves several people. Implicating both protagonists and transforming them, this exchange is not a matter of one recognizing the other; both are part of a process that will leave neither unchanged. All of a sudden the "other" is no longer a stranger. Although a person might initially position himself as "other," he only truly becomes other through the process of a transforming recognition. We can take as proof of this the force possessed by claims to equality and equal citizen status, claims that are always present, albeit at times disguised, but that nevertheless remain the common value to which we can always appeal, however violent the conflicts. In summary, modernity is less an unbending and predetermined way of life and more a process of acquiring shared references, thereby transcending even our most radical differences. This is what Touraine proposes as the "primary space," the focus where the process of living together is elaborated.[11] This primary space is subjective, but the subjects are not immutable, they are in the process of a transforming recognition.

It's impossible to fix a time limit on this transforming recognition or to confine its risks to some circumscribed area. Our forms of organizing recognition politically and socially only deal with one aspect of things. The transformation we are talking about overflows their limits, seeps into other aspects of existence, and ultimately affects all domains. Recognition fosters upheavals, engenders resistance, affecting areas we considered private until now. Recognition challenges identity, even challenges how I recognize my own identity.

Is it any surprise then that fear raises its head? Fear of the other and their difference: conceiving the relation to others only in terms of domination and violence is something deeply ingrained in humanity's collective memory. Humans nevertheless do meet, commingle, and continue giving birth to new humans: mestizo children.

What about *Mestizaje?*

Mestizaje is a perfect illustration of violence transformed. Multiculturalism without *mestizaje* doesn't exist. People sharing the same territory meet. They commingle and mix languages, customs, symbols, bodies. They give birth to something more than themselves: children whose origins will be different from their own. Only an imposed violence like apartheid can prevent this process. *Mestizaje* is the continuance of multiculturalism.[12]

But handling *mestizaje* is tricky. It has bad press. It's easier to talk about mestizo and *mestizaje* when they concern others, as if accepting difference and recognizing a mixed heritage were somehow dangerous. The word itself is looked on suspiciously: the suspicion attached to admixtures, disorder, impurity, to all that is unclear, concealed and, in the end, risky. *Mestizaje* is the unavowed part of multiculturalism.

"Somos mestizos"; the smiling man before me seemed to imply that these two words were sufficient to summarize his entire existence. Pride and self-assurance were equally perceptible in his attitude. We were in Mexico and I was hearing the words for the first time. After many years, I came to understand the force of affirmation and vindication contained in this identity and the price paid for it throughout history. What had occurred in the past and was still going on in Mexico, what the word *mestizo* designated—wasn't it the dramatic encounter of cultures? The most violent of the Indian traditions, the Aztec, mixing with the Spanish, Europeans whose religious expression had also assumed the most violent of forms. At the dawn of modern times, this encounter, suturing the earth, stands as both atrocious and revealing.

The first meaning of *mestizaje* corresponds to the precise experience of the colonization of the American hemisphere. Consequently from the very beginning, the word is associated with the idea of race and domination. Hence its ambiguity and its negative side. As Nathalie Zemon Davis writes: "I use the word 'Mestizaje,' while fully recognizing that this word, like the word hybridity, are connected to a world dominated by racist thinking."[13] With its positive side, however, it designates a decisive aspect of the human adventure—a commingling, a weaving together of human beings. To quote Nathalie Zemon Davis again:

> Strictly speaking, "Mestizo" ordinarily designates children born of a clear-cut ethnic difference. But Mestizaje may also represent a culture, an intellectual world attached to Mestizo families or milieus, or attached rather to the choices these families and milieus have made and to the experience of emigration and voyage.[14]

This is the contemporary way of speaking about *mestizo cultures* and of *cultural mestizaje*.

The original meaning and the current meaning resonate together but today the word has new amplitude. It's worth examining this issue and investigating the word *mestizaje* to better understand the contemporary situation. It is worth the effort to grasp more precisely the historical experience of Latin America and how it can act as a litmus test for the intermixings that multiculturalism brings about in our societies, thereby establishing an interaction between the strict meaning and the broad sense of *mestizo*. The initial experience that took place on the American continent and today's multicultural experiences are in no way identical. Neither the age, nor the place, nor the styles of encounters are identical. And yet, they have some essential aspects in common: the encounter between human beings in all their otherness; the encounter's violence and singularity; the emergence of new identities through the transformation of cultures; the stakes of a transforming recognition. Pursuing our investigation of the word *mestizaje* will make it possible to perceive how the encounter of cultures continues, this inevitable and necessary encounter that makes humanity, in the lovely words of Rene Depestre, a "métier à métisser."[15]

Notes

1. Amy GUTMANN, Preface to Charles TAYLOR, *Multiculturalisme, difference et démocratie* (originally: *Multiculturalism and the Politics of Recognition*), translated from English, Paris, Aubier, 1994, pg. 9 of the preface.

2. Ibid., pg. 15.

3. Charles TAYLOR, op. cit.

4. Charles TAYLOR, op. cit., pg. 37.

5. Charles TAYLOR, op. cit., pg. 38.

6. Charles TAYLOR, op. cit., pg. 72 (The quotes from C. Taylor are reproduced from *Multiculturalism and the Politics of Recognition*).

7. Michaël WALZER, *Commentary*, in Charles TAYLOR, op. cit., pg. 131

8. Joël ROMAN, "Un multiculturalism à la française," in *Le spectre du multiculturalisme americain, in Esprit*, June 1955:

> L'épouvantail du multiculturalisme américain est périodiquement brandi en France à chaque nouveau débat de société. Nous serions ainsi menacés d'un avenir de communautés fermées sur elles-mêmes ne patageant plust aucune valeur commune et qui seraient autant de prisons pour les individus.

9. Cf. Michaël WALZER, *"Individus et communautés, les deux pluralismes,"* in *Esprit*, op. cit.

10. Joël ROMAN, op. cit., pg. 151. Regarding the entire debate, see: under the direction of Michel WIEVIORKA, *Une société fragmentée? Le multiculturalisme en débat*, Paris, La Découverte, 1997:

Peut-être serait-il possible de corriger quelque eu les tendances centripètes de la société française en lui injectant quelques doses de multiculturalisme, tandis que la société américaine souffrirait d'un tropisme centrifuge inverse et gagnerait peut-être à s'inspirer de notre tradition réplublicaine.

11. Alain TOURAINE, *Pourrons-nous vivre ensemble? Egaux et différents*, Paris, Fayard, 1997.

12. The statistical figures in this field are difficult to interpret. Current estimates are that today 2.5 percent of the world's population is mestizo. The situation is very different according to the countries and the continents. Cf. *Encyclopaedia Universalis*, article *Métissage*.

13. *Le Monde*, June 19, 1995.

14. The figures on migrations and population shifts give an idea on the potential situations of cultural *mestizaje* in our societies. Thus in 1990, 5,897,370 people were living in France who had not been born there, representing 10.4 percent of the population. This is a higher percentage than for the United States or Germany, but lower than for Canada. (Source: Poitiers University, Centre d'étude des migrations, http//www.mshs.univ-poitiers.fr/migrinter.)

15. Rene DEPESTRE, *Le métier à métisser*, Paris, Stock, 1998.

CHAPTER THREE

~

The Vocabulary of *Mestizaje*

The meaning of *mestizo* and its derivatives is currently undergoing transformation. Up until the middle of the 1980s, the word was hardly used in France. It was mainly in the vocabulary of specialists or was occasionally used to designate out-of-the-ordinary situations, such as an exotic marriage or birth. Now its use is becoming almost commonplace, and it can be found in the language of documents and also the arts, fashion, and in plain, everyday life. The expression *mestizo culture* crops up frequently in reference to the theater, films, or dance, and a "colored" world is prevalent in advertising. Neighborhoods of large cities are referred to as "mestizo." Outlooks and thinking are also "mestizo": *mestizaje* becomes a value and carries with it new resources.

What does the current change in vocabulary signify? It is a new word, or at least a new way of using the word. Like a sentinel, it is trying to attract our attention and wake us up to what is happening around us and that which we don't always know how to see. The word seems to search for how to position itself in our conversations: looking backward to evoke a lost world, or looking forward as if to a promising utopia. And what if there were a position from which it could designate an undreamed-of present?

The Vocabulary of Marginality

A word from the past, charged with nostalgia for some (suffice it to mention the success of films or novels romanticizing "colonial" times), the word *mestizo* at first calls up a lost world, the world of Europe colonizing the planet and discovering the color of far-off populations. This vision includes eye-catching colors, pleasure, but also a cynical game that shamelessly covers up the violence of colonization. Colonial literature portrayed the mestizo as an intermediary, sufficiently close to be trusted, yet ready to betray, and sufficiently distant to be abandoned without qualms, rejected without regrets. An exotic word that inherits all of the ambiguity contained in the situation of the person engendered through an encounter between two groups separated up until then by time and space. A word from some far-off other place, that can only occasionally impinge upon the established, solid universe of quotidian Europe.

It's a short step from the exotic to the pejorative. For a long time the word was suspect. And it still is. Designating someone or something as mestizo is already alerting one's listener that we are dealing with an unclear situation, with something ambiguous, with a person or a reality not totally trustworthy. A quick look at our usual idioms is proof enough. The word *mestizo* and the words associated with it carry, in our countries and most of the time, a pejorative meaning.

A few years ago, going from Mexico to the United States, I was talking with a Mexican American businessman and, unsure of my English, I asked him at one point: "How does one say 'metis' (mestizo) in English?" He looked at me in surprise, paled, and after some dumbfoundment, answered: "There isn't any word in English." All the words he then proceeded to enumerate were in fact pejorative: half-breed, hybrid, mixed-blood, half-caste, even bastard. And he concluded: "In the language I use for work and that my children use in their daily lives, I have no way to communicate the reality of my identity." It's true English speakers like Americans don't have a precise word to designate the same thing that makes their neighbors, the people of Mexico, so proud.[1] While *mestizo* connotes pride to the South, to the North anything mestizo elicits mistrust and violence. Despite the efforts accomplished, Mexican Americans, and with them all "colored" people, remain the people that dominant ideology, as well as language, relegate to society's margins.

The investigation is worth taking further, and it has been taken further in the principal languages, particularly English and German, by a linguist who, studying literature and dictionaries, has attempted to collect the different connotations of the word and the various designations of the mestizo reality.[2] In German as in English, there exists no specific word to depict the human reality of *mestizaje*, and the words usually employed to translate the word *mestizo* are borrowed from the animal or the mineral world and always have a negative connotation. Witness in German the noun *der Mischling* (hybrid) and the adjectives *vermischt* (mixed) and *mischblutig* (mixed-blood); also *der Blending* (bastard), "which reinforces the stain of dishonor and discredit by association to it a correlative taken from the terminology of morbidity."[3] Translations corroborate these findings. In both languages, no specific word exists and the words used are of a deprecatory nature. No doubt of course that the transcription of the original word is making its appearance in both languages: *der Mestize* in German, mestizo in English. But this use is recent and still restricted. The richness of the word as it has come to exist in the Latin American countries is in no way to be found in German or English.

The word's pejorative nature goes back very far. The word was coined in the Middle Ages and comes from the low Latin *mexticuis*, "born from a mixed race," itself derived from *mixtus*, mixed. It is principally said about things rather than people. For example, a metal, *fer metis*, or kinds of food, *vin metis* and *pain meteil*, made from wheat and rye. *Fabric* is *metis* when it is woven from two different fibers, linen and cotton. *Metis* designates mixture, impurity. And even if the mixture is appreciated (metis fabrics are known to be more solid and preferable for household use), the word is deprecatory from the start. Its etymology encapsulated this pejorative connotation.

After looms, we have agriculture and husbandry, where the word designates crossbreeding of plants or animals in order to improve their characteristics. The classic example is the mule, a cross between a donkey and a mare—a word that will later turn up in *mulatto*, an adjective applied to humans to designate a person born of a white parent and a black parent. Most dictionaries are content to apply this word to plants and animals, and the extension of the word can be closely followed in their succeeding editions. Thus the Littre' (1877) and the Larousse (1880) dictionaries only give examples of animals (sheep) and plants under the words *metissage* and *metisse*. [4]

However, the same 1877 edition of the Littre' mentions a social usage of the word beginning in the twelfth century. It can designate individuals of low birth or a misalliance. And from the sixteenth century on, the word will apply to Indian/Spanish children, with the meaning that it receives during and after the large colonial conquests. Montaigne, Voltaire, Buffon, and all classical literature use this meaning. It must be remarked, however, that even then in its social human usage, the original sense of the word, associated with animals, and its pejorative connotation are never far off.

Thus we have a word that for a long time was relegated to the margins because it designated an experience itself considered marginal. An experience referring either to the animal world or to humans, in this case taking on a figurative meaning connoting ambiguity, admixture, impurity. As demonstrated by Patricia Schutz, the word is associated with the idea of bastard, that is, illegitimacy. The mestizo is someone whose birth contravenes the law, is illegitimate, someone who shouldn't be here. That's why it designates what occurs elsewhere, at the frontiers of humanity, on the fringes of the infra-human, among animals, or in distant new lands. A murky word whose attraction derives precisely from the elusive nature of the reality it names, simultaneously attractive and dangerous.

This word today is making a strong comeback, bringing with it both fears and fascinations. In summary, this word, still rarely used despite advances and almost forbidden in daily conversation, is an alarm. Raising the subject of *mestizaje* is getting close to a danger zone, a suspect area, one of those subjects that aren't mentioned in polite company. The word will travel a long road before it gets a positive connotation and designates one of the richest facets of the human adventure. The story is worth telling.

The Scale of Colors

The word widens its scope during the sixteenth century, with the Portuguese colonial expansion (Brazil, *mestico*), then the Spanish one (*mestizo*). It no longer applies merely to individuals but to entire groups. When Cortez conquers the Mexican Empire with a handful of men, the toll taken on the indigenous populations through the violence of war but also because of the new maladies introduced by the Europeans nearly results in the disappearance of the Indians. Shrewd man of politics, as unscrupulous as he is self-serving, Cortez sees only one solution to the demographic catastrophe. Intensive *mestizaje* will be the instrument for populating first New Spain, then the rest of Latin America. A new people is born in pain and grief, between quasi-slave labor and organized rape. As we are reminded by the inscription on the *Plaza de las tres Culturas* in Mexico City: "Here, on August 13, 1521, heroically defended by Cuauhtemoc, Mexico Tlatelolco fell into the power of Hernando Cortez. It was neither a victory nor a defeat, but the painful beginning of today's Mestizo Mexico."[5] This is no longer about something foreign and exotic but about one of history's most violent and somber pages (even if there were a few exceptions to the general atrocity), yet also one of its most grandiose pages because in that violent beginning, an entire people recognizes its origins and the source of its identity. Mexico clearly and strongly affirms itself mestizo.

At the same time, in this beginning is also rooted the fundamental contradiction of Mexican society, Octavio Paz writes:

> The ambiguity of the Creole was multiplied by two for the Mestizos: they were neither Creole nor Indian. Rejected by both groups, neither the social structure nor the moral order ascribed them a place. For the two traditional moral standards—the Spanish one founded on honor and the Indian one founded on the family—the Mestizo was the living image of illegitimacy. . . . The Mestizo was literally a man without any status.[6]

"Without status," "illegitimate," "outside the moral order." The mestizo is someone inferior. In the new order emerging, he represents a radical threat of disorder and disintegration. It's essential therefore to pin mestizos down, to determine who is mestizo, who is more or less marked, "stained." Social exclusion and physical appearance are conjugated. From the very start, the mestizo's body is labeled, marked with an identification that will follow him or her all through life. An identification that will determine a mestizo's place in society and with whom he/she can associate. Consequently, mestizos will be fated to feel either shame or pride. For the mestizo is simultaneously the outcast, the dangerous threat, and the standard-bearer of the future. As Octavio Paz underlines:

> Among all the groups composing the population of New Spain, the Mestizos were the only ones to truly incarnate this society, its true sons. They were not, like the Creoles, Europeans who were trying to grow roots in a new land; nor were they, like the Indians, a part of the landscape and a prehispanic past. They were what was really new in New Spain. Even more: they were not just what made New Spain new, but what made it other.[7]

Now the scale is inverted. Color is no longer suspect but becomes a source of pride. Social order is subsumed and sublimated into a cosmic order where the mestizo can claim a privileged position, one of greater proximity with the earth as nature's privileged go-between. The word *mestizo* acquires more breadth. It indissolubly conveys violence and life. It encapsulates the human element, but taken to its paroxysm, the inescapable cruelty is revealed, but also the revitalizing and subversive power. Mexico's poets, authors, and political leaders have constantly explored this theme. Mexico testifies to the entire universe that the wound out of which it was born has borne fruit, human fruit, mestizo fruit still undergoing transformation.

During a visit in Mexico one day to an old, established family, the head of the family showed me all the portraits of his ancestors hanging on the walls. His lineage went back, so he told me, to the first colonial viceroys. He added: "*The whole history* of the country is summarized in our family." The person with me whispered in my ear: "*Except for the Indian part.*" My companion was a man proud of his mestizo identity. And he suddenly made me aware of the subtle line of demarcation to be found within a mestizo society. This society doesn't claim homogeneity, indeed it established differences and creates dividing lines that classify and set up a scale of *mestizaje* based on hypothetical proportions of white blood and Indian blood. And the degrees of this scale are purportedly visible in the color of the skin or in facial features!

The modern age, in Europe and America, will thus develop an arithmetic of colors, starting in the sixteenth century and continuing through centuries of colonization. A person's color is presumed to correspond to the proportion of the two bloods he/she possesses, and this proportion to the degree of *mestizaje*. Magnus Morner established a list of these degrees. He analyzed their subtle nuances,[8] translating them into words claiming precision and indicating an individual's place on the scale of *mestizaje*. Thus we have the mixed bloods, the half-bloods (mestizos), quadroons, and octoroons. Every country, every idiom concerns itself with this question and constantly comes up with new vocabulary. Even so, everyone is familiar with the vocabulary and through language, a correspondence is established between biological origins, skin color, and social position.

Mestizaje thus becomes a means for classifying human beings and determining the power plays between them. Skin color becomes an element of power. A classification is established that makes power coincide with the degree of *mestizaje* and hence, a greater or lesser degree of threat or power. Pride or contempt will translate, in daily interactions, the fears or fascination, and also the repressed violence or the assurance power gives. Turnarounds in the situation, like the mestizos taking power at the time of the Mexican revolution, only reinforce and illustrate this scale, inscribed in the collective unconscious as well as in bodies.

Mass *mestizaje*, triggered by the conquest of the American hemisphere, puts both American and European societies and their varying reactions to the other to the test. History thus translates and etches into the events that take place, the attitudes, values, and symbols to a large extent dominating it. And the adventure of *mestizaje* is revelatory of the prohibitions, the acceptances, and the refusals upon which Western societies are built and that they have imposed on the rest of the world to their profit. For, at the top of the scale is to be found the white man, hated and envied, endowed with all the privileges of humanity and civilization. The Grand Larousse dictionary still writes at the end of the nineteenth century: "No one will contest that the white race is superior to all the others."

Another word crops up at this point: *race*, associated with the word *mestizo*. Starting in the eighteenth century, it will justify the scale of color and power. It is a word with a strange history, beginning in the Middle Ages when it designated a lineage or a group of the same generation. Starting in the sixteenth century, *race* also acquires a dual signification, simultaneously glorious—when it means lineage, and particularly a noble lineage, and pejorative—when it designates a class of suspect people. This positive/negative ambivalence continues, and in France, for instance, the use of the word *race* is problematical, while in Mexico *la raza* connotes pride and designates the people. Buffon, and in his wake the nineteenth century, will classify human races by skin color, perpetuating in western imagination the junction between the biological and the social. As we note above, all young Europeans were familiar with this scale of colors in school.

The way the words link is evident: color, race, power. This equation will become a determining factor in the construction of the modern societies stemming from European colonization. From that point on, the politics of intermixing—encouraging it, or on the contrary prohibiting certain unions—becomes an instrument of power used with a view to precise ends. Human desire, the attraction between men and women, sexuality and its fruit, the child, are controlled, valued, or rejected, as the powers that be see fit and in function of their imposed will on the group. For these authorities, the relationship to the stranger and the commingling of people, or of the races in the broad sense of the term, become a subject to be regulated by political law, by the law of the Empire.

From Contempt to Recognition

Mestizaje is appraised according to the equation color = race = power. Even today it often continues to have the negative connotations described above. Use it and the frightening vision of a world full of violence, intolerance, and lies looms up, given that for Europeans in modern times, the birth of mestizo children and the appearance of mestizo populations were the consequence of colonial conquests. The latter were inaugurated in the sixteenth century by two catastrophes: the destruction of Indian civilizations and the enslavement of Africans, catastrophes whose effects continue to be felt and which have played a part in shaping our societies. Without these two catastrophic occurrences, our contemporary world would not resemble what it does, the people inhabiting the planet would not have the identity they do, the culture of our modern countries would not be what it is. Even forgotten, even denied, they are at the root of what we pride ourselves on, at the heart of the modern age's very fiber, like a secret, hairline fracture weakening the loveliest of facades.

Using the word *mestizo* and its associated words means alluding to that flaw beneath appearances and suggesting that our splendor rests on a price others have paid. For this reason, this word cannot fail to provoke ill ease in contemporary westerners. With this word, there suddenly arises all the weight of past violence and injustice. Despite our policies discourses and neat charts and diagrams, we can suddenly glimpse what is unexpected and imprecise in our immense human complexity. It's like a child we are ashamed of and would prefer to hide. Its existence is a sort of primal wound in modernity, that no remedy seems to be able to heal. And thanks to the flawed logic that so often throughout history identifies the victims with the guilty, mestizos are vaguely considered to be marked by the stigmata of these faults. They are living witnesses to this primal wound. Hence the suspicion accompanying the vocabulary of *mestizaje*. And in fact, the adjective *mestizo* still too often appears pejorative to people who are not used to using it or hearing it.

But a turnaround in the situation is happening. Situations referred to as mestizo are multiplying and gaining increasing acceptance. Hope is infusing the words used to speak of mestizo reality. These words are accompanied by liberty and invention. They name what is new and exciting in our societies. No surprise then that art is one of the primary fields where this reversal is perceptible. Mestizo cultures, mestizo music, mestizo films, and festivals, the list is long. These encounters enrich each day with their innovation, fresh experiences, and vitality. To give just one example, the newspaper *Le Monde* recently published a long article, "The Fertile Mestizajes of Talvin Singh," presenting this London singer: "Where the Indian continent meets hip Albion, that's where you can find Talvin Singh, a pioneer among Asian youth attempting to reconcile their traditional culture with their passion for today's music." *Le Monde* quotes him:

> I grew up feeling that music was a unique and identical language. I've never taken seriously the hierarchy established between "serious" music and popular music. I've always adored the sounds and styles born in the streets and in the youth cultures. I've steeped myself in all styles: pop, acid house, techno, just as much as in Indian music. I baptized my album "OK" because this word is a synonym for universality.[9]

Here's the nexus of this profound reversal. The words of exclusion and segregation become the words of universality. The same is true for situations, experiences, in short all that makes up culture. Words are being invented every day, and more than words, so are languages, rhythms, and melodies. And ways of speaking, dressing, films, and novels, advertising, fashion, architecture. There is not a field in one way or another that isn't becoming mestizo. The old arithmetic of colors is blown away, assigned roles lose their footing. The marginal becomes the center. The word *mestizo* is being charged with radically new meaning, emotion, and potential.

Reversal: from contempt to recognition to acclaim. Stemming from a racist context, the "mestizo" and the words of *mestizaje* become instruments in combating racism. They attack it on the territory from which it sprang forth: exclusion and inequality.

Such a reversal of the situation is a sign that mestizos are recognized. They and only they can transmute the meaning of words and their connotations. As with Martin Luther King Jr. proclaiming "Black is beautiful," they can erase the color scale and declare it dead. They can transform how we see things and give new value to words up until now pejorative. The revenge of the mestizos, one can say. Not a political revenge content to simply inverse roles and make the dominated the dominators. What is happening is ever more subtle and human, a cultural transmutation, meaning a shift at the symbolic level. Such is the irony of history: what was rejected now assumes its place at the heart of innovation, as with jazz, a hundred years ago, when these slave rhythms not only became identified, in the eyes of the entire planet, with the culture of their masters but also with invention and vitality. In spite of, and through, violence, the recognition of a shared humanity arises from the midst of this reversal.

> Humanity, if it intends to survive, needs to find a new way of dealing with cultural differences. This is where the Mestizo's contribution resides today: through his very being, he demonstrates that a racial mix need not necessarily lead to destroying a cultural nationality, but that it can even help to build such a cultural nationality.[10]

The word *mestizaje* and associated words, redefined, can help us more than any others to designate what the stakes are in the multicultural situations of our societies. It has the advantage of focusing attention on what is dynamic in the processes at work. Its multiple itineraries indicate how identities are forged, diversity born, and also at what price. It acts like a revealer of what for a long time was ignored or rejected. By using it as a reference, in the shifting ground between past experiences and today's capacity for invention, it becomes possible to shed new light on what is involved in contemporary multiculturalism.

Notes

1. See for example, *Le metis culturel*, Internationale de l'imaginaire, Nouvelle serie, n 1, Paris, Maison des cultures du Monde, 1994.

2. Patricia SCHUTZ, Dire le metissage, paper presented at the University of Metz, Department of Literature, 1995.

3. Ibid., pg. 10.

4. The indications given here are taken from various dictionaries, entry-word Metis. See: Emile LITTRE, *Dictionnaire de la langue fransaise*, Paris, 1863–1876, and Pierre LAROUSSE, *Grand Disctionnaire du XIX siecle*, Paris, 1866–1876. See also Alain REY, *Disctionnaire historique de la langue fransaise*, Paris, Dictionnaire Le Robert, 1992.

5. "Aqui el trece de Agosto milquinientos veintiuno, heroicamente defendido por Cuauhtemoc, Mexico Tlatleloloco caio en poder de Hernan Cortes. No fue Victoria ni derrota, sino el doloroso comienzo del Mexico mestizo de hoy."

6. Octavio PAZ, *Sor Juana Ines de la Cruz, ou les pieges de la foi*, Paris, Gallimard, 1982, pg. 53:

L'ambiguite Creole se redoublait chez les metis: ils n'etaient ni Creoles no indiens. Rejetes par les deux groupes, ils n'avaient place ni dans la structure sociale, ni dans l'ordre moral. Face au deux morales traditionnelles- l'espagnole fondee sur l'honneur et l'indienne fondee sur la famille—le metis etait l'image vivante de l'illegitimite. . . . Le metis etait litteralement un homme sans position.

7. Octavio PAZ, op. cit., pg. 54:

Parmi tous les groupes qui formaient la popilation en Nouvelle Espagne, les metis etaient les seuls a incarner reellement cette societe, ses veritables fils. Iis n'etaient pas, comme les Creoles, des Europeens qui cherchaient a s'entaciner dans une terre nouvelle; pas davantage, comme les Indiens, une realite donnee confondue avec le paysage et le passé prehispanique. Iis etaient la vraie nouveaute de la Nouvelle Espagne. Et plus: ils etaient non seulement ce qui la faisait nouvelle, mais autre.

8. Magnus MORNER, Le metissage dans l'histoire de l'Amerique Latine, Paris, Fayard, 1971 (translated from English). Also, Hugo Tolentino, *Origines du prejuge racial aux Ameriques*, Paris, Robert Laffont, 1984 (translated from Spanish).

9. Cf. *Le Monde*, October 3, 1998:

> J'ai grandi avec le sentiment que la musique etait un seul et meme langage. Je me suis toujours moque des echelles de veleur entre musiques savante et populaire. J'ai toujours adore les styles preoduits par la rue et les cultures jeunes. J'ai baigne dans tous les genres, la pop, l'acid house, la techno autant que la musique indienne. J'ai baptize mon album OK, parce que ce mot est synonyme d'universalite.

10. Virgil ELIZONDO, op. cit., pg. 147.

~

CHAPTER FOUR

Mestizaje Recognized

Mestizaje is an integral part of the human adventure's long term. It evokes perspectives and stakes broader and richer than our immediate situations; it refers to mechanisms preceding them and to dynamics underpinning them. These mechanisms and dynamics make *mestizaje* the convergence point for the broad orientations that have shaped, and continue to shape, humanity. They remind us that humanity is engendered through the encounters of bodies, that its survival depends on a constantly renewed capacity to overcome exclusions, and that human desire has an unlimited future. Evoking *mestizaje* amplifies the contours of our present situations. Underneath these situations resonate long-term currents whose control escapes us and whose implications reach further than our spotty, partial comprehension of them. Perhaps it's our murky perception of these mechanisms, or a fear of the stakes they imply, that makes certain debates so sharply acrimonious. I've repeated the experience a hundred times: bring up *mestizaje* in front of a group of people and immediately different reactions shoot forth, going from virulent rejection to intrigued surprise to enthusiastic interest. Each person confusedly senses that in taking a position on *mestizaje*, they are also taking a stance on a direction for humanity.

Bit by bit, the work of anthropologists and biologists reconstructs how things reached their present state, whereas only poets are capable of sketching the outlines of an unknown future. Both scientists and seers consider *mestizaje* a fact that has shaped the human adventure.

Inescapable Diversity

How did humanity get to its present-day point, where appearances attest to enormous diversity yet where at the same time people share a common membership in humanity? Anthropologists and biologists use the term *hominization* to describe the process by which humanity emerged during the course of evolution.[1] And the entire history of the life sciences, from Darwin until today, accumulates discoveries and sparks new explorations. In his book, *De le Biologie a la culture*,[2] Jacques Ruffie retraces how biological research arrived at its present state of facts and conclusions. The vast panorama he describes sheds light on different aspects of the complex evolutionary process leading to the genesis of human beings. A decisive point for this research occurs with the advent of genetic analysis methods that radically renew the study of human diversity.

> Ever since Broca, the notion of race has underpinned traditional anthropology. The discovery of inherited factors in the blood has made it possible to apply to the human species methods of genetic analysis of populations. The results clearly show that no such thing as races exist in humankind.[3]

Traditional anthropology, up to and including the so-called "scientific" racism of Nazi Germany, considered *race* the key for classifying humans. Human diversity was a function of different races considered autonomous. These races, each with its morphological characteristics, formed ensembles in which existed a correspondence between morphology, psychological aptitudes, and moral tendencies considered innate to each group and unaffected, except occasionally, by environment or education.[4] These views led quasi-biology. Within this framework of thought, *mestizaje* could not fail to be considered a degeneration.

The research of the last half-century has completely invalidated this way of looking at things. This research provides no base for claiming that differences between humans are founded on alleged racial differences. There is no hierarchy of races, as there are no human races. Blood is the same for everybody everywhere; it is impossible to invoke purity of blood in order to justify differences or hierarchy of any sort. All human beings are part of the same family. As a result, the concept of race is not a cogent one for organizing human diversity. Even if some people persist in granting it some interest for the purposes of classification, we are forced to recognize that this concept is difficult to define biologically, surrounded by confusion, and of little help in understanding human evolution. Jacques Ruffie uses the concept of "de-raciation":

> De-raciation has become an irreversible phenomenon. Humanity, after having been polytypical over a very long period of time, is now in the process of becoming monotypical. The differences between whites, Asians, blacks, or the more subtle increasingly nebulous, represent nothing more than sequels from the past. And from a very distant past because, for a long time now, probably since Neolithic times, the movement of racial diversification has been reversed: homogenizing forces are stronger than the forces of differentiation.[5]

Plus, ideological connotations adhere to the concept of race. In the background still lingers the idea of one race's superiority over the other, of one group's over the others. The ambiguity kept alive around a link between morphology and cultural characteristics doesn't stand up to scrutiny. Even less plausible is the idea that this correspondence is innate. Modern anthropology over the last fifty years has profoundly modified earlier ideas and proven that the differentiation of populations is cultural and not racial. It has "pulverized the notion of race."[6]

Understanding human diversity can be done only by using totally different means, infinitely more nuanced and discerning, highlighting within a common biological given the differentiations occurring at multiple levels and going beyond the so-called demarcations of so-called racial groups. Human diversity is more a function of culture than of biology, because individuals, through their activities and knowledge, build their own future. The dividing line is thus not between distinct races, reputedly genetically different and explaining human diversity. This line runs between ever-more diversified cultural choices, representing so many ways of appropriating our common biological given and using it as a starting point for achieving all of humanity's "possibles." To quote Jacques Ruffie:

> Almost all the populations surrounding us are the result of multiple intermixings.
>
> Each of us is someone's Mestizo. Mestizaje has accelerated through the course of history to the point where in modern times, it has attained a scale hardly imaginable.[7]

In effect, modern life has given impetus to the phenomenon, "Due to modern life, the human species increasingly tends towards homogenization . . . it corresponds to a fundamental tendency among living beings."[8] According to Ruffie, humanity is going toward generalized "cafeaulaitisation" (from the French *café au lait,* coffee with milk, having a uniform, beige color), meaning neither indeterminate blending nor uniformization. "Cafeaulaitisation" is a way of explaining differences and forging diversity by giving them a better grounding than in the myth of race. The word *race* is hence emptied of any biological signification. On the other hand, the commingling, the *mestizaje,* between different human groups, and no longer between allegedly pure races, gains acceptance.

From the biologist's point of view, what we have here is a dual shift: first from the idea of a pure race to the idea of diversified groups ceaselessly pursuing a process of diversification. *Mestizaje* designates this process. Second, from biology to culture. *Cultural mestizaje* designates the passage from one to the other, or better yet, represents where they interface. At this point, *mestizaje* acquires a positive meaning and scope. Not only is it impossible to erect barriers between people in the name of race, skin color, or the alleged natural superiority of one group over the other, but even more importantly, the attention given to human beings' biological reality invites, for the present and the future, wide recognition of the fact that they are mestizo. That is to say, they are people who are caught up in an ongoing process of the commingling of individuals and groups, and this process is the condition for survival and a chance for the future. In this way, biology unequivocally settles the matter of the ambivalence in the concept of *mestizaje.* For biology, there is no doubt that *mestizaje* is positive.

On the other hand, as Ruffie recognizes, it is not up to biology to resolve the considerable problems posed to societies and cultures by *mestizaje*. We are forced to recognize that *Mestizaje* has occurred more often than not through violence, especially in the modern age with its migration and slave trade. This is where biologists hand the problem over to sociologists.

To be complete, we'd almost have to convoke all of the social sciences that concern themselves with studying diversity among human groups and how it comes about. Not that the concept of *mestizaje* is considered a key one for sociology. Occasionally used, especially in South America, to designate this to that group, it is not considered an analytical category.[9] It neither possesses elements that could serve to elaborate a theory of society nor operative concepts to uncover social mechanisms. *Mestizaje* remains a descriptive, evocative word, not a theoretical concept. It was used for a while by the "culturalists" but quickly abandoned because it conveyed a rigid view of culture and revealed itself too blurred around the edges for the purpose of analysis.

Nevertheless, *mestizaje* lingers on the fringes of the thinking in sociology. Every now and then the word is used by someone trying to name with an all-encompassing word what analytical categories tend to dissect. Ethnologists and anthropologists use it readily. What attracts their attention, including Roger Bastide's, are the "mestizo cultures" that he still calls "cultures in transition." What he is interested in is conceptualizing how encounters between distinct groups and their culture are brought about. "The only object of study we ever have are complex, pluri-ethnic societies, and it is these societies we have to analyze along with their different forms of sociability."[10] He endeavors to understand "what happens when two different cultures encounter each other."[11] His favorite terrain, Brazil, allows him to develop a set of concepts designed to understand the mechanisms at work. Distancing himself from North American culturism, he gradually abandons the concept of *syncretism* and substitutes the concept of the "interpenetration of civilizations." Thus the concept of *acculturation*[12] neither designated an indistinct, disorderly mix nor the mere borrowing of some cultural elements by another culture. It refers to the elaboration of a new set of elements making it possible to live in two worlds and to go from one to the other by establishing associations.[13] What results is not confusion but a process of substitution of one element for another depending on which world an individual is in. In this way, the behavior of an Afro-Brazilian "changes depending on which world he is in, since he belongs to both. What is sometimes decried as a black's duplicity is really the sign of a great sincerity on his part. If he seems two-faced, it's because two faces do exist."[14] This is what Bastide calls "the *discontinuity principle*" ("principe de coupure").

Attracted by confines, Bastide nevertheless wonders: can what he has observed in Brazil be transposed to other places, in particular to Europe? His answer is increasingly *yes*. For him, the encounter of civilization continues to happen, producing a new civilization, and the contemporary world is experiencing a multiplication of acculturation situations. In each case, it's important to place the diverse elements in the global context of societal phenomena, which today include ideologies as well as political and economic choices. "The task of contemporary anthropologists in this field is distinguishing the different sorts of dialectics that can be established between cultural contacts and social contacts, between the interpenetration of civilizations and the integration of ethnic groups into national groups."[15]

Nevertheless, the fact that he frequently uses the word *mestizaje* can be taken as an indication that it is more expressive than technical terms like *acculturation* or *interculturality*, in the same way that it expresses more than the concept of multiculturalism does, as we've seen. In fact, it is on a different level—more physical, less intellectual—than the others. This word is all-encompassing and evokes the experiences of actual men, women, groups in a way that directly involves their identity, their way of saying "I," of answering the question: "Who am I?" To quote Bastide again: "Culture is an abstraction. It's not cultures that are in contact but individuals who are interacting."[16] We're not looking at an object called "culture" but at the trajectories of individuals and groups searching for their identity.

This is the reason for the disparity existing between the analytical work of biologists, anthropologists, sociologists, and the winding trajectories of *mestizaje*—this kind of disparity is generally the case between theoretical analysis and the way a phenomenon is perceived and experienced by the people it touches. This discrepancy creates a space where the work of transforming oneself and the world can occur. Biologists reject the fatalism associated with the concept of race and draw attention to the "rootedness" in the body of all humanity, while at the same time, thanks to Bastide and others with him, the manifold ways human groups interlace are taking shape before your eyes. These different fields form something like what we could call the coordinates of *mestizaje*, helping us to "locate" it. *Mestizaje* is indeed acculturation, multiculturalism, it is played out in the body, in culture, and in polity. It's all that and more too. It indicates what precisely no analytical category can seize in its entirety: the will to self-expressive existence in all of its unique distinctness. This will fuels the processes and the dynamics in/of the different groups and is fundamental for individuals as well as in societies. In this inventive, fluid space between rational concepts and unique existences, new individuals and groups are forged, and exchange and *mestizaje* pursue their movement. No one can say where *mestizaje* is going. Except poets.

A Desired Totality

Poets have long been way ahead of other thinkers. They intuitively know there exist no barriers between the races, that human differences are enriching, and colors are destined to weld into a bright rainbow, not into dim grey. In literature, we can follow the theme of the intermixing of human groups. As soon as humans write, the stranger/foreigner's presence becomes a primary theme, because it is inevitable. The warrior, the seductress, or the lovely captive are there on the edges of all discourse exalting the group. They are the other, different, part of the landscape and without whom it's impossible to exist or define oneself.

In his controversial book, *Black Athena*, Martin Bernal takes to its extreme limit his defense of the thesis of the mestizo origin of Greek culture, indeed of Western culture.[17] According to him, the idea of a pure Hellenism, representing the ideal and the standard of all civilization, was an idea invented by the scholars of the nineteenth century, particularly by Germanic thinking. However, in the author's view this model doesn't hold up to facts, nor to the analysis of population shifts, nor to study of the origins of language. He follows the convoluted evolution of this "Aryan model" for culture. Like everybody else, the Greeks are the product of intermixings and continually undergo this process of intermixing. Their roots are in Asia and Africa, particularly in Egypt. Even though Bernal's demonstration may be systematic, it has the advantage of pinpointing an inevitable question. Why do humans, the fruit of multiple intermixings—true for individuals as well as groups—always tend to deny their mixed origins, both in language and thought? Mestizo in fact, why are they so reticent to acknowledge it in words?

In the twentieth century, Cesaire and Senghor, to name only the great, break the taboo on the words of *mestizaje* and sing the melody of negritude and the mingling of colors. Although the entire oeuvre's music should be heard, we'll have to content ourselves with a few words.

> How well I know that the blood of my brothers will once again redden the Yellow Orient on the edges of the Pacific Ocean raped by tempests and hatreds. How well I know that this blood is the Springtime libation which the Grand Publicans have been using for seventy years to fertilize the lands of Empire.[18]

And:

> New York ! New York, let black blood course through your blood. Similar to an ointment of life, may it lubricate your articulations of steel. May it grant your bridges the curve of hips and the suppleness of vines.

Also: "My Portuguese blood lost its way in the ocean of my negritude."[19]

In answer to the question: "Why do you write in French?," the poet replies:

> Because we are cultural Mestizos, because although emotionally and sentimentally we are Negroes, we express ourselves in French, because French is a universal language of refinement and honesty."[20]

Here we are: the amplitude of a boundless dream, violent confrontations, the language honed to express the novelty of the message. Through his words, Senghor opens up our hearts and minds to today's reality of *mestizaje*, since for him: "All great civilizations have been civilizations of Mestizaje."

Let's conclude with Michel Serres, a scholar who can also be a poet at times. He constantly alludes to the concept of *mestizaje*, which he considers the key for education. As he writes in *Le Tiers-Instruit*:

Apprenticeship consists in this very kind of Mestizaje. Strange and original, a mix of genes from his father and mother, the child evolves
uniquely by way of these new intermixings: all pedagogy repeats the
child's procreation and birth: born left-handed, he learns to use his right
hand, remains left-handed, is reborn right-handed, where the two directions intersect: born a Gascon, he remains and becomes French, in reality Mestizo: French, he travels and becomes Spanish, Italian, English,
German; if he marries and learns their culture and language, he's now a
quadroon, an octoroon, soul and body commingled. His mind resembles
Harlequin's cloak. This is equally true for raising the body and for educating. The Mestizo here is called the educated-third.[21]

Mixed, intermixing, intersection, harlequin's cloak; *mestizo* suggests all
these things simultaneously. It can't be substituted for by any other
word because it contains and affirms what each of the other words ver-
balize. Their significations seem to converge in it. But *mestizo* signifies
more: it gives each of the words a richer sense than held by their primary signification. *Mestizo* is more than mixed, more than an intermixing or an intersection and much more than a cloak, be it harlequin's. Michel Serres holds the word's many facets up to the light and
evocatively plays with them. But he's careful not to give a definition,
and in his way goes deeper into the question, "What *does* this word represent?" If only for a moment, let's freeze its harlequin twirling in an attempt to glimpse in which direction the words of *mestizaje* are pointing,
what they are trying to designate to our distracted attention.

Between Body and Dream

Mestizaje is a slippery word indeed, changing meaning and scope with
changing situations. As Francois Laplantine and Alexis Nouss remark:
"Since we can't pin down what Mestizaje is. . . . We can at least attempt
an approach by saying what it is not. Not a declaration, not an assign-
ment of a role, not substance, not principle."[22] Any definition effectively risks giving just one aspect of a swirling situation. Bastide, for instance, stresses how *mestizaje* concerns "social races." He closes in on it
like this: "The Mestizo is a person who, because he/she has ancestors of
different colors, is defined as such by society and to whom is consequently assigned a specific status."[23] This kind of "definition" can be

perfectly pertinent in some situations. But Bastide goes on to remark in the same article that in the United States, if a person has a black ancestor, that person is considered black, while in South America, having a white ancestor makes a person white. In other words, the notion of color in both cases is difficult to pinpoint and moreover, as we've seen, holds no signification from the standpoint of biology. Where does one establish boundaries in this human kaleidoscope?

So, here we have a word that can be understood in the broadest sense, since in a way, everybody is mestizo, and yet at the same time, a word of the narrowest designation, since it fastidiously uses a bizarre arithmetic to distribute the mixes up and down a scale of purity. It's a word locked into a very specific history—the centuries of modern European colonialism—yet at the same time, a word in which authors recognize a fundamental phenomenon of the human adventure. A word associated with the body, and yet more capable than any other of opening to poets the gates of dreams and aspirations.

In short, *mestizaje* is a word lightly skipping along over the range of meanings, from the narrowest to the broadest. A word moving from one field to another, from a continuously changing biological field to the social and the cultural fields. So that, the oft-used expressions "biological *mestizaje*" and "cultural *mestizaje*," even though they seem pertinent in the context of our ordinary experience, don't stand up to scrutiny. For, where does one place the "biological" dividing lines between who is and who isn't mestizo? Similarly, at which point can one start talking of "cultural *mestizaje*"? Plus, the expression goes between an older, "biological" pole to a "cultural" pole clearly acknowledging its mestizo nature. Two asymptotes as it were. The conclusion we risk arriving at is that everything is considered mestizo. In that case, the word would lose its pertinence and be emptied of all signification.

In truth, as we noted before, the word's signification is in the process of changing. Why such renewed vigour for this word, if up until now it's been so liability-laden? In the author's view it's because it represents the conjunction of three elements that the usual language and ways of thinking tend to disassociate: difference, mixture, body.

Difference. In the case of *mestizaje*, impossible to mask or deny because it's visibly inscribed in body. The other is different for me. The others are different from what we are. Difference is simultaneously fascinating and frightening. Hence, the two-step of attraction/repulsion. Tzvetan Todorov subtitles his book on the conquest of America, *The Question of the Other*.[24] This is indeed the crux of what came into play during the history of the North American continent, and is still being played out. *Mestizaje* sheds light on the dual movement of fascination and fear when faced with the other, in this case the Indians. Christopher Columbus's letters abound with expressions of admiration. On Indian women: "Every one was beautiful. We could believe we were seeing the stunning naiads or the fountain nymphs celebrated in Antiquity." He goes on: "These people are the finest and the most peaceful in the world."[25] Initial texts are full of this kind of language. But wonder will become nightmare and engender the violence we know. *Mestizaje* makes difference visible. It makes it manifest, inscribed in the body's physical features, to be identified and labeled by everyone. And *mestizaje* perpetuates difference, since once the alleged purity of bloodlines has been transgressed, the future generations will be marked by this "fault." Hence the implacable arithmetic we noted earlier. As if, at all costs, it were necessary to measure the difference, in order to conjure it.

But a difference acknowledges and invites encounter. And social order and thinking are constantly preoccupied with organizing this encounter, defining its limits and predicting its effects. Now, a mestizo encounter creates a certain disorder. It's an unpredictable "weave," and badly woven at that, from the viewpoint of the established order. In other words, it introduces a dose of the unpredictable, like a hole in the fabric of society. Consequently, for a long time and in many eyes it did not represent a real encounter but a contemptible intermixing, synonymous with disaggregation, the threat of dissolution and death. We aren't talking here, however, of just any mix. It's neither a breaking-up into separate parts, lethal indeed, nor a utopian fusion. "A middle road between micro-division and fusion, Mestizaje as a concept could aid us in our reflections and analyses concerning the contemporary world's crises."[26] This middle road leads to mestizo "philosophy" and thought, according to the authors.

Indeed, it is a potentially fertile mix, a fertility linked to the body. To speak of *mestizaje* is to be reminded that human beings emerge from a biological grounding that it's not up to them to erase. Humans are obligated, by speaking of *mestizaje*, to determine their place using the coordinates of time, space, and body in which their destiny is inscribed. To speak of *mestizaje* is to place humans squarely in front of the particularisms without the loveliest intellectual constructs. It's an invitation to situate anew each culture within its potentialities and its limits, if we want the discourse on interculturalism to be more than a mere evasion. To speak of *mestizaje* is to designate the work cut out for interculturalism: revise, interpret, and render livable all of the different aspects of human experience.

Underneath the debate over *mestizaje* runs, like an invisible river, the long-term adventure of the advent of human beings and their millennia-old evolution, fuelled by the strength of their desire. *Mestizaje* appears as a kind of crystallization of the important stakes in the encounter between humans: difference, intermixing, and the body. This is perhaps what renders every debate so ambivalent, injecting it with an ample measure of humanity and passion. Raising the subject of *mestizaje* means raising the questions of human evolution, the body and desire. No surprise then that in recent times the first to recognize and give *mestizaje* a role in their reflections and analyses were anthropologists, biologists, and poets. Human beings are a mix, an encounter of diverse elements constantly reassembled, bodies and genes, heart and mind, societies and civilizations. *Mestizaje* embodies one of the fundamental, because founding, dimensions of the human adventure.

So why then does *mestizaje* remain suspicious? Why is it kept on the sidelines? Referred to only reticently? For we have to admit, our gallery of championing authors unites a few important voices, but they are far from being the entire chorus. They are more the discrete strains of flutes and violins than the booming of trumpets and horns. What is habitually more often heard are the well-assured voices of groups affirming a strong, clear identity exclusive of others, groups exalting their vigour, their superiority, affirming their unchanging identities and their position as unfailing heirs of the glorious traditions of their ancestors, unerringly perpetuating humanity's everlasting, undecaying adventure.

Probably we are becoming more prudent. At the end of our twentieth century, we are only too aware of the massacres occasioned by these kinds of claims to purity. But even if we accept the commingling of individuals and groups as an unavoidable fact, our thinking on the subject remains a bit short. The old categories still influence too heavily our ways of thinking. We continue thinking of identity in terms of simili-tude, tradition in terms of reproduction and the encounter of groups in terms of controlled exchanges. *Mestizaje* is an invitation to break out of this vicious circle's trap. Human cultures, and individuals too, cannot remain glued to a mirror reflecting an unchanging sameness. For this reason, recognizing *mestizaje* means also unreservedly recognizing what is organically present in human cultures: the possibility of innovation.

In this we hold the key to the relation between the narrow sense and the broad sense of *mestizaje*, or between two expressions whose limits we've mentioned: biological *mestizaje* and culture *mestizaje*. One does not necessarily entail the other. In other words, there is no immediate and automatic relation between biology and cultural intermixing. Sim-ply having parents of differing ancestry is not sufficient to guarantee the child will effortlessly partake of both cultural heritages. A thousand other factors intervene, beginning with education and personal histo-ries. We are aware for instance of the suffering and tenacity that the search for one's origins, real or supposed, can generate in people whose faces or bodies indicate an origin different from the culture of their adopted country. We see this desire to know in children from other continents adopted early and raised in Europe by European couples. This is indeed proof that although the connection between biological *mestizaje* and cultural *mestizaje* is not automatic, there can exist a rela-tionship between them.

This relationship assumes the form of a search for identity, one's own and that of the groups to which one belongs or desires belonging. This search is organized around the three elements we've seen: difference, encounter, and the body. In this way, a constant to-and-fro between the two poles—biology and culture—may be established. One could be the face or the metaphor of the other. To summarize, *mestizaje*, in its nar-row, biological sense, reflects the cultural encounters accelerating be-fore our eyes. Today, ideas and cultures are mixing, the way bodies com-mingled in the past and still do. What is evidenced in one field can help us to understand, and offer analogies for, what is happening in an-other field. From one pole to the other a thousand ties are created, through folklore, legends, and history, political structures and symbolic schemas. We need to identify them. They attempt a recognition of *mes-tizaje*, an expression of its human reality between the body and dreams.

The plane had barely landed. The person waiting for me immediately settled me in his car and we drove to the center of the city. In the
humid summer evening, I was dazzled by the immense quadrilateral and
the sumptuous monuments I was discovering: Mexico's Zocalo Square.
"You see," he told me, "we didn't know if we should put up a statue here
to Cortez or to Montezuma. So we left it empty."

The empty square. The emptiness of Mexico's square is structured.
The large, Spanish-style square, designed by Cortez, is bordered by the
National Palace, with Cortez's home, the cathedral, and now, the recently discovered sumptuous ruins of the *Templo Mayor* close by. But in
the center of the immense space, there is just an open area. Nothing,
except perhaps all the possibles, all the potentialities, which no representation can hope or claim to circumscribe As unpredictable as a
child. All this is what the word *mestizaje* designates. I was just beginning to discover it.

Notes

1. Cf. Henry de LUMLEY, *L'Homme premier*, Paris, Editions Odile Jacob,
1998. According to the author, "the anthropological characteristics of the current human groups were defined as soon as the Mesolithic" (pg.192), i.e.,
around 10,000 years before our era.

2. Jacques RUFFIE, *De la biologie a la culture*, Paris, Flammarion, 1976.

3. Ibid., pg. 375:

Depuis Broca, c'est sur le concept de race que repose l'Anthropologie tradition-
nelle. Le decouverte des facteurs sanguins a conditionnement hereditaire a permis
d'appliquer a l'espece humaine les methods d'analyse genetique des populations.
Les resultants demontrent clairement que chez l'homme les races n'existent pas.

4. Ibid., pg. 443 sq.

5. Ibid., pg. 413:

Le deraciation est devenue un phenomene irreversible. Tres longtemps polityp-
ique, l'humanite tend a devenir monotypique. Les differences entre les blancs, les
juanes, les noirs, ou celles plus subtiles, qui subdivisent encore ces groupes fonda-
mentaux er don't les fromtieres sont de plus en plus floues, ne representent que les
sequelles du passé. Et d'un passé tres lointain car depuis longtemps, depuis sans
doute le Neolithique, le mouuvement de diversification raciale est inverse: les
forces d'homogeneisation l'emportent sur les forces de differenciation.

6. Ibid., pg. 406.

7. Ibid., pg. 414:

Presque toutes les populations qui nous entourent sont le resultat de multiples croisements. Nous sommes tous les metis de quelqu'un. Ce mouvement n'a fait que s'accelerer au cours de l'histoire pour connaitre dans les temps modernes une ampleur a peine imaginable.

8. Ibid., pg. 375.

9. It's noteworthy that today linguists are once again referring to the concept of *mestizaje*. Cf. Bernard HUE (Director), *Le metissage du texte, Bretagne, Maghreb Quebec*, Rennes France, PUF, 1995.

10. Cf. Roger Bastide, *Encyclopaedia Universalis*, article "Acculturation," 1/104.

11. Cf. under the direction of Philippe LABURTHE-TOLRA, *Roger Bastide ou le rejouissement de l'abime*, Paris, L'Harmattan, 1994.

12. *Encyclopaedia Universalis*, op. cit., 1/102–107.

13. Cf. Denys CUCHE, "Le concept de "principe de coupure et son evolution dans la pensee de Roger Bastide," in Laburthe- Tolra, op. cit., pg. 69 sq.

14. Maria Isaura PEREIRA DE QUEIROZ, "principe de participation et principe de coupure, la contribution de Roger Bastide a leur definition sociologique," Archives de Sciences Sociales des Religions, 47/1, January- March 1979, pg. 152.

15. *Encyclopaedia Universalis*, op. cit., 107/a.

16. *Encyclopaedia Universalis*, op. cit., 103/c.

17. Martin BERNAL, *Black Athena, Les raciness afro-asiatiques de la civilization classique*, Paris, PUF, 1996.

18. Leopold Sedar SENGHOR, *Priere de paix, a Georges et Claude Pompidou, Oeuvres poetiques*, Paris, Le Seuil, 1990, pg. 91:

Je sais bien que le sang de mes freres rougira de nouveau l'Otient Jaune, sur les bords de l'Ocean pacifique que violent tempetes et haines. Je sais bien que ce sang est la libation printaniere dont les Grands Publicains depuis septante annees engraissent les terres d'Empire.

19. Leopold Sedar SENGHOR, *Saudades*, op. cit., pg. 117:

New-York! Je dis New-York, laisse affluer le sang noir dans ton sang. Qu'il derouille tes articulations d'acier comme une huile de vie. Qu'il donne a tes ponts la courbe des croupes et la souplesse des lianes.

Leopold Sedar SENGHOR, *Saudades*, op. cit., pg. 166: "Mon sang portugais s'est perdu dans la mer de ma negritude."

20. Leopold Sedar SENGHOR, *Le poesie de l'action*, entretien avec Mohamed Aziza, Paris, Srock, 1980, pg. 61:

Parce que nous sommes des metis culturels, parce que si nous sentons en negres, nous nous exprimons en francais, parce que le francais est une langue a vocation universelle, que notre message s'adresse aussi a des Francais de France et aux autres homes, parce que le francais est une langue de gentillesse et d'honnetete.

21. Michel SERRES, *Le Tiers-Instruit*, Paris, Francois Bourin, 1991, pg. 86–87:

L'apprentissage, consiste en un tel metissage. Etrange et original, deja mélange des genes de son pere et de sa mere, l'enfant n'evolue que par ces nouveaux croisements: toute pedagogie reprend l'engendrement et la naissance d'un enfant: ne gaucher, il apprend a se servir de la main droite, demeure gaucher, renait droitier, au confluent des duex sens: ne Gascon, il reste et devient Francais, en fait metisse: Francais, il voyage et se fait Espagnol, italien, anglais, Allemand; S'el epouse et apprend leur culture et leur langue, le voici quarteron, octavon, ame et corps meles. Son esprit ressemble au mantraus d'Arlequin. Cela vaut pour elever les corps autant que pour instruire. Le metis ici s'appelle le tiers-instruit.

22. Francois LAPLANTINE, Alexis NOUSS, op. cit., pg. 80.
23. In P. BESSAIGNET, *Encyclopaedia Universalis*, Article "Metissage."
24. Tzvetan TODOROV, *Le Conquete de l'Amerique, La question de l'autre*, Paris, Seuil, 1982.
25. Ibid., pg. 42.
26. Francois LAPLANTINE, Alexis NOUSS, op. cit., pg. 68.

~

CHAPTER FIVE

A (Hi)story of
Desire and Violence

History is inscribed between the body and dreams. History makes it possible to organize survival and traces the trajectories of desire, scarring time with its violence. *Mestizaje* runs through the entire weft of history. It's not incidental to history. It accompanies conquests and discoveries and cannot be separated from the major human migrations. These migrations mix populations. Wars, migrations, deportations blur or erase geographical and social reference points and force people to survive, albeit for an unpredictable future. Such events oblige people to live elsewhere and differently, in the middle of strangers with whom intermixing slowly occurs. History's glorious side shows a parade of conquerors. The latter, however, can only advance men and women, displaced, uprooted, deported, forced to be part of the great mixings of populations that give time its density. Desire and violence intertwine. History blends into them a dose of *mestizaje*.

It can't be denied that societies have constantly been preoccupied with *mestizaje*. Whether it's imposed by necessity, like Cortez in order to populate America, or rejected out of ideology to maintain some illusory purity or safeguard a few interests, no society has been able to ignore *mestizaje*. Except by remaining outside of history, that is, isolated from other human beings. We find its trace in the epic poems and legends translating the aspirations of different populations, as well as in the critical writings of historians revealing the undertaking's painful reverse side.

Mestizaje haunts history both as aspiration and as terrible wound inflicted by a permanent violence. Writing a history of *mestizaje* would be tantamount to rewriting the human adventure's unfolding. But some great figures emerge—as mythical as they are historical—who, in the collective consciousness, designate the stakes of this adventure and push these stakes to their extreme limit. They are emblematic figures of what continues unfolding before our eyes today. We'll have to content ourselves with evoking two of these figures, separated by eighteen centuries, who wanted to meld populations.

The Flesh of Empires

The Empire—meaning in the broad sense, a centralized and imposed political power—exists only through its will to mix populations. Whether it means to or not, the Empire becomes the melting pot of *mestizaje*. The latter supplies it its substance, its flesh. Soldier, merchant, laborer, or slave, the mestizo is the Empire's flesh. But from Alexander the Great's empire (336–323 B.C.) up through modern colonial empires, this intermixing will be regulated in several manners. With, however, one point in common: the Empire exists only by creating and maintaining inequalities between the groups it is made up of. As a result, it's possible to trace the relation between *mestizaje* and inequality throughout history. The mestizo is accepted, even promoted, but only on the condition that he/she remains inferior.

Alexander first. At the dawn of Western history, Alexander is reputedly the first—at least so say his traditional biographers—to have installed *mestizaje* as a model, the first to have made it a project enshrined in a determined, political decision. Initially, his conquest had an immense ambition, we are told: uniting East and West. It was something of a philosophical project, since Aristotle's student wanted to put into practice the universal vision his teacher had imparted to him. His project proceeds from this line of vision, and the conquest is simply the embodiment of his civilizing enterprise. Thus Gustave Droysen who, at the beginning of the nineteenth century, inaugurates a revival in historical studies on Alexander and becomes the poet of this epic.[1] Everything is presented as unfolding according to an inescapable logic: Alexander's expeditionary project, its confirmation by oracles, his consecration by Egyptian gods, and the apotheosis of his marriage to Roxane. Quoting Quintus Curtius:

> Consumed by the flame of his desire, Alexander ordered the bread to be brought forward, according to the customs of his country. For Macedonians, this is the most sacred symbol of carnal union. The bread was halved with a sword and each spouse ate a piece. In this manner, the king of Asia and Europe was united in marriage to a captive who would bear him the child who would command the conquerors.[2]

In this way the encounter of populations was perfectly accomplished, since Persians become Greeks, and Greeks Persians, and from the union of Macedonians with women of the Orient would be born the new, universal race of humanity. "The union of the Hellenistic and Asiatic worlds—with its advantages and its drawbacks—was founded for centuries." As events occur, whether negative or positive, they are all evaluated in light of Alexander's project. For example, the marriages at Susa, where ten thousand Greek men wed an equal number of Persian women. Another example: the revolt at Opis. There was a lot of grumbling and threatening among the Macedonian veterans, probably weary but more likely jealous of the newly arrived soldiers, who were granted privileges making them the equals of the veterans. Alexander turns the situation to his favor. During an opulent feast, he declares that everyone is like a member of his family for him and that he looks upon each one with equal consideration. He prays for concord and a sense of shared community, Koinonia, between the victors and the vanquished. The veterans returned to Greece, bringing with them a new spirit.

Thus, here would have existed in the history of humanity one grace period when, thanks to the genius of one man, unity and universal spirit were achievable in perfect equality among men. The words *concord, collaboration,* and *peace* are repeatedly used by the ancient authors. They also frequently mention a respect for law and tradition: "The Persians were impressed that he (Alexander) did not hasten to satisfy his desire, but wanted to respect all the forms and customs of their country."

Maybe. Contemporary historians are less enthusiastic. Their critical study of sources and their methods of interpretation inspire them with prudence. Clifford Bosworth observes: "There is no allusion to Alexander's envisioning a hybrid master race formed by the two people, nor that he considered humanity to be a brotherhood under his universal leadership."[3] He adds in a note:

> The prayer during the reconciliation ceremony was a practical, almost cynical way of reducing the tension that Alexander had exploited for his own profit. In fact, policy didn't change. The Iranians continued to be dominant, at least numerically, in the army while the positions of power at court and in the satrapies continued to be monopolized by the Europeans. A shared sense of community in the Empire remained no more than wishful thinking.

We're far from Droysen and his shining epic. Whatever the truth may be, no one can deny that "Alexander provoked a mutation in the Antique world. His expedition fundamentally transformed relations between Greeks and barbarians."[4] Alexander is open to many interpretations, even the most contradictory. But beyond the undisputed historical events, beyond the multiple interpretations, whose views and relevancy are open to discussion, there remains what Alexander set in motion. Whatever the events that took place at the junction of Europe and Asia during the fourth century B.C., they are the reference point for what follows. Rome and the Western Empire, the kings of France and Napoleon see in Alexander the forerunner of their dream. Even the Nazis will abusively try to use him as justification.

Alexander's glorious deeds still resonate in the stories that even today keep his legend alive. Fantasy or promise, the idea of humanity's brotherhood haunts us. In its name, adventurers embark, soldiers march, merchants justify their trade. Alexander's dream dominates history as an ideal toward which we must strive. Let's retain for our purposes a few aspects of this legend, aspects we will encounter anew: the desire for unity, the destruction of borders, the role of women. Decisive elements that provide a framework for the empire's project and in which *mestizaje* plays an inevitable role.

At the other end of time, we encounter this epic again, but in a far-different context and conducted in a far-different manner. Eighteen centuries later, the Europeans to the north of the Mediterranean undertake a new expansion at the time of the great discoveries. Cortez (1485–1547) epitomizes the Conquistador, strategist, clever empire-builder, and pitiless politician all rolled into one. But his is a different universe from Alexander's.

Alexander's universalistic vision is absent from Cortez's project. Like the other conquistadors, Cortez is mainly motivated by the promise of riches and a taste for adventure. First a colonist in San Domingo, then prospector for gold and a notary, he enters the service of Cuba's governor, Diego de Velasquez, and has a falling out with him followed by a reconciliation before Velasquez makes him a proposition to lead an expedition to Mexico: a third expedition since the first two, in which Cortez did not participate, had failed. Cortez, conscious that his protector distrusts him and wants to relieve him of his command, sets sail without informing Velasquez on February 18, 1519.

He reaches Mexico as the representative of the businessmen who bankrolled him, not as the Cuban governor's. Nothing here of a vast, universal aim. Nevertheless, upon his arrival, Cortez turns to the king. A dual allegiance to God and king will henceforth constitute the horizon of his endeavor. He writes to Charles the Fifth and proclaims his desire to evangelize the new populations. All the conquistadors share these traits. We could consider this as just part of the ideology of the day, too often the servant of personal ambitions. But in doing so, we would be improperly transposing our own conceptions to a far-different era, a time when the supreme values were a sense of honor and a desire to serve. In his letters to the king of Spain, Cortez explicitly refers to these values. His personal project, cloaked in this grandiose vision, is now part of a greater project. The latter rapidly becomes universal: conquering the entire world for the honor of God and the king of Spain. Like all projected empires, the conquest of the New World is grounded in universalistic intention.

The way the project unfolds is well known and we won't delve into it here but pick out the aspects observed in Alexander's undertaking. First of all, the intermixing of populations. The encounter with the Indians was absolutely and completely unprecedented. Tzvetan Todorov is right in affirming that it was more bizarre and strange than the conquest of outer space was for us.[5] He gives us a remarkable analysis of the mutual discovery between the Spanish and the Amerindians, a discovery that will open the door to *mestizaje*. What Cortez wants, unlike the other conquistadors, "is not to take, but to understand." In other words, the Conquest will become for him a matter of "signs." Hence he simultaneously organizes the Conquest's war tactics and creates a peacetime colonial policy. In this way, he is different from all the other conquistadors and rises above them. In his letters to the king of Spain, he goes into detail about his conquests and the implementation of his policies. These policies aim at making the Indians his majesty's subjects. They aim too, once Mexico is destroyed and Cuauhtemoc assassinated, at dividing the Indians among the different estates, the *encomiendas*, to work for the Spanish.

The Conquest was far from tender, but Cortez and his men esteemed their enemies. The multiple negotiations he had with various groups in order to make allies of them bear equal witness to his respect and his shrewdness. But Cortez, and therein lies his genius, rapidly becomes conscious of the amplitude of his undertaking. It's impossible for the immense territories conquered to be populated and exploited by a handful of Spaniards. So *mestizaje* becomes a necessity. In this case too it's a matter of building an empire. Political aims make their own use of the Conquest's violence. Imposed *mestizaje*, with or without marriage, is its tool. The Spaniards wed Amerindian princesses, as Cortez weds Malinche. But even though, as has often been remarked, racial discrimination is unknown at the beginning, it is nevertheless true that the European is at the top of the ladder and the Amerindian at its bottom. The Amerindian wife is the object of violence and her children rejected by their foreign father. America becomes the land of *mestizaje*, and of modern *mestizaje*, that is, a *mestizaje* not only linked to political will (this was also the case with Alexander) but a *mestizaje* engendered through violence and connoting contempt.

For the Conquest is not just about military superiority and the Spanish imposing themselves through superior weapons and tactical skill. It's also a biological catastrophe, and this is probably even worse for the indigenous peoples since they are condemned to short-term death because of the illnesses introduced by the invaders. The Conquest signifies the collapse of a world: the world of men and of gods. Better than evoking the atrocities endured, a poem like the "Plea of the Aztec Sages" affords a glimpse of the radical violence that walled the Indian in silence: "Allow us to die, allow us to perish, since henceforth our gods are dead."[6]

The modern signification of *mestizaje* is born in Spanish America. Inscribed in the word is the memory of this violence, the price paid for the Empire's development. Cortez's glorious epic rests on this ugly reverse side. Hence the Conquest's ambiguity. It is simultaneously death and life, painful and glorious, destructive and future-facing. As the above-quoted inscription states on Mexico City's Plaza de Las Tres Culturas, it is "the painful beginning of today's Mestizo Mexico." Three cultures: the Indian, the Spanish, and the mestizo, born of the two others. Modern *mestizaje* thus reveals itself as profoundly ambiguous; inevitable, carrying the seeds of the future, linked to violence.

Malinche epitomizes this ambiguity. Slave and princess, she surmounts her situation through her role as a facilitator of communication. She's the one who translates into the indigenous idioms the words of her lord and master. She is at the crux of the encounter between two peoples completely foreign to each other, and it's actually rather surprising that the image of her that has reached us expresses fully and clearly this carnal/intellectual duality. Here is what Cortez's first letter says about her:

> The Indian chief of Tabasco had made him a gift of twenty Indian women. Among them was a women of noble condition, well-proportioned and whose beauty could pass for rare. . . . She was baptized some time later and given the name of Marine. . . . She spoke many languages and explained to the Indians in the language of Mexico, to Aguilar in the language of the Yucatan, Cortez being obliged to wait while his words circulated in this fashion until Marine had learned Castillian.[7]

Princess, translator, she will, while remaining true to Cortez, attempt to protect the native peoples in one of the greatest catastrophes ever to befall humanity. Repudiated, she will live out her life in pain and sorrow. But she will never betray Cortez. A fascinating figure full of sorrow, she inaugurates the history of modern Mexico and remains a legendary figure of *mestizaje*.

Legendary Figures

Malinche, Roxane; the figures to which *mestizaje*'s memory attaches itself are feminine ones. Legendary figures, they are like luminous dots in the canvas of days and, at the same time, their stories revive lacerating injuries. They help to support history and also to make some sense of it.

Such is Roxane. She has indeed become the symbol of the union of all peoples. The Persian princess whom Alexander wed represents, we are told, the first known attempt to make *mestizaje* an instrument of universality. From this perspective, *mestizaje* introduces a new norm: a *mestizaje* actively chosen, we could say, and seen as bearing the seeds of humanity's future. Differences of race and culture become positive elements and a way of furthering the full realization of individuals and groups. The universal is thus within reach, in the here and now of inter-ethnic encounters.

Alexander's Empire embodies a new conception of the link between peoples. It's no longer the Greek city-states that represent the elementary political unit, it's the Empire's subdivisions. The world is enlarged and the frontier moves toward the Orient, to India, with the hope of one day going beyond. To this extension of space corresponds a different political organization. The model centered on the city-state closed to barbarians is replaced by the Empire, a new space of diversity and unity, subject to a prince's despotic, even if at times benevolent, power. The former barbarians have an accepted place in it. Exchanges between different territories now occur, drawing the outlines of a new known world, from the Mediterranean to the heart of Asia. Rome will just need to place its steps in Alexander's footprints.

As a kind of counterpoint, it is worth recalling another figure of antiquity. In collective imagination, Dido, the legendary queen of Tyre, represents, as it were, the antithesis of Roxane. Strictly speaking, Dido precedes Roxane by a few centuries since the founding of Carthage is habitually thought to date from the end of the ninth century B.C. Elissa-Dido in collective memory is the woman who refuses to unite with the other, the foreigner. She is the wanderer who doesn't procreate in a foreign land.[8] She is a powerful figure whose symbolic importance runs through antiquity as well as through the modern history of the Western world. For Virgil, she embodies a negative figure destined to highlight Rome's glorious destiny through her own tragic one. Rome, a conquering, intermixing, assimilating empire, like Alexander's; an empire believing from the start in its universal mission. Carthage, self-centered city strewing the coast with mercantile counters, only interested in trade. Rome, one of whose founding events is the rape of the Sabines and "whose children," Virgil tells us, "are both Trojan and Latin." Carthage, whose founding princess refuses marriage with the indigenous King Iarbas in order to preserve the integrity of her new homeland and who will consequently remain childless. Her destiny leads her to death, as Rome eventually puts an end to her city and builds an empire. An empire that accepts all peoples, but more importantly, offers everyone the possibility of benefiting from the same privileges, thanks to the concept of citizenship. This is the innovation ushered in by Rome.

> With you, "Roman" is a word no longer belonging to one city but designating a kind of collective race, and not a race like the others but a sort of counterpoint to the others. Today, you don't separate races between Greeks and barbarians, but you have divided peoples between Romans and non-Romans. . . . Nevertheless, envy does not reign in your empire. For you were the first to give fully and not in bad grace, since you made all things available to all men and granted everything to those capable of not being subjects but masters.[9]

Mestizaje, instrument of universality, invites a citizenship going beyond the borders between clans. Everyone can become a citizen, even an emperor, of Rome, "the common Fatherland of the world." But the empire survives only on violence and inequality. It's this last point that Christianity will defy. Christianity preaches a brotherhood that is not merely the brotherhood of the masters, but that recognizes masters and slaves as equals.[10]

We evoked Dido simply as a counterpoint to Roxane. For the latter, as for Malinche, her true story is less glorious than her legend. The destiny of Alexander's son, as well as his mother's, was tragic. Both Roxane and her son were assassinated by jealous heirs of the great king. Frontiers once again divided off portions of the empire which rekindled their quarrels. The dream faded, until it was seized anew by others. But the vision remained of a land harmoniously unified thanks to the intermixing of peoples considered equals. *Mestizaje* became the instrument of universal realization, if only in dreams.

At the other end of history, Malinche is a sort of reverse echo to Roxane. She is also a figure of *mestizaje*, also essential to the empire's development. But it is an empire less idealized than Alexander's empire and a *mestizaje* far more violent. There is nothing here of the climate of wonder surrounding Alexander's epic adventure, nothing even of the solemnity of marriage rituals; just violence in its most extreme forms, rape and slavery.

> The symbol of the painful fracture is Dona Malinche, Cortez' Indian mistress. It is true that she willingly submitted herself to the Conquistador who, once she had ceased being useful to him, forgets her. Dona Marina, to use her Christian name, has become a symbolic figure of Indian women: fascinated, raped or seduced by the Spanish.[11]

It's understandable from this point of view that "the Mexican people cannot forgive Malinche her betrayal." A figure of *mestizaje*, she is also an inaugural figure of the violence which for centuries submerged Latin America. The slave trade and the enslavement of Africa followed the collapse of the Amerindian world, and have marked to this day the continent's tragic destiny. At the dawn of modern times, Malinche personifies all the anonymous cases of *mestizaje* that bloodied, as well as forged history. There is a malediction associated with her that tends to cast a shadow on or contaminates her. No wonder then that a few years ago, when the authorities of Coyoacan near Mexico City wanted to erect a public monument to her, public outcry forced them to abandon their project.[12] *Mestizaje* is inevitable, but also impossible to bring out into the open.

The Labyrinth of Contradiction

The Empire breaks apart because of *mestizaje*. Impossible to acknowledge, impossible to deny, *mestizaje* brings out into the open the contradiction sapping the Empire, the secret fault line on which the entire construction rests. The Empire is postulated on the idea that its universalistic project on one hand, and individual aspirations on the other, are one and the same, or at least that they converge—and that harmony and goodwill regulate their relations.

In reality this is not the case. Between the Empire's objectives and the multiple desires of the individuals or groups composing it stands the Empire's law. A law that is often summarized in one expression: the prince's will. Texts on Alexander refer to his *despoteia*, his total and arbitrary power. Of course, he does exercise his power benevolently. This *despoteia* showers benefits on the prince's subjects and also on the conquered peoples. Alexander creates cities, educates the Persian children as Macedonians, and constantly recalls the common dream of unity and communion whose strongest symbol is marriage. The effect of such a benevolent reign is indeed to put each person in their place, a place chosen for them by the conqueror.

Consequently, the way in which the Empire accomplishes its project is by installing distinctions and creating norms. It traces boundaries between territories and between clans. With an eye on its interests, the Empire accords privileges and favors or distributes punishments and prohibitions. It assigns individuals or groups their roles and places in a perfectly unequal way, and every now and then decides to celebrate unity and universality with a military or religious ceremony. This was the case with Alexander and it was also the case in Spanish America. Each person is thus assigned an identity by the law of the Empire and finds him or herself in the designated place.

Individual desire is thus harnessed and exploited by an endeavor over which people have little or no control. Conforming to the designations and divisions established by the Empire, the condition for accomplishing its project, appears for everyone to be the condition for the accomplishment of their own desire. Compliance with this view is a point of honor for each individual. The law of the Empire becomes at that point the means of realizing both individual and collective destinies. Because naturally, the collective project is presented as corresponding to everyone's desire. To sum things up, the social body and the desiring body are considered as corresponding, if not coinciding. This is the nexus of the Empire's force, of its capacity to assimilate and to dominate.

But this way of realizing the Empire is also a way of alienating those to whom it promises its benefits. Such is the law of the Empire. A great many of the people building it reap the benefits only in the very long run, if ever. The law of the Empire contains this contradiction but masks it at the same time. The law imposes order and channels desire, and by the same token mutilates it. The three legs on which the Empire stands—its universalistic project, its inegalitarian order, and its imposed identity—sacrifice desire. Desire is condemned to remain in the place assigned it by the Empire: reservation, ghetto, or ethnic community. The Empire keeps a grip on the groups by separating and opposing them. Such is the price to be paid for the peace it brings and also for the mediating role toward the universal that it wishes to play.

Now, the mestizo's existence reveals for all to see the contradiction inherent in such a project and denounces this contradiction. The mestizo child's very existence is effectively the revelation of desire and its impossible-to-hide fruit. It is a desire emerging from the bosom of societal links, creating a certain disorder; a desire that transgresses all the separations and role assignments that the empire diligently tried to put in place. Alexander might have attempted to profit from and partially control encounters between Persians and Greeks, but this was not the case for modern colonialism, where exclusion and taboo prevailed. So, desire reappears in its most brutal form, the radical violence of rape. Consequently, desire directly challenges the order imposed by law.

This is why the law rigorously attempts to keep the mestizo child in the margins and even keep him or her from being born. It doesn't know how to make a place for this child, and can't. Socially, the mestizo doesn't fit into a category. He can only be excluded, discredited; even his social position makes him an outlaw. He internalizes this discredit as shame. The mestizo is rejected by everyone. Octavio Paz describes this perfectly:

> The Mestizo was the living image of illegitimacy. His sentiment of illegitimacy fed his insecurity, his perpetual instability, his see-sawing from one extreme to another, from courage to panic, exaltation to apathy, loyalty to treason. . . . In a society where the division of labor coincided even more so than in others with the social hierarchies, the Mestizo was literally a man of no position.[13]

What's more, the transgression of *mestizaje* is reinforced by the fact that the child is the fruit of the masters, that is, the guardians of the law. The law is betrayed by the guardians of the law. Cortez gives us a savory illustration of this. In his fourth letter to the king of Spain, he requests of the king some appropriate help in order to evangelize the Amerindians. After suggesting that a few bishops be sent over, he changes his mind, "preferring zealous priests to bishops who'll be occupied in obtaining good positions and other favors for their children and who'll dissipate their wealth in vainglorious pomp."[14] The reason for his change of opinion is simple: "If (the Amerindians) knew that we call ministers of the living God people who indulge so indecently in excess, irregularities and profanations, they could not fail to scorn both the religion and its priests." The violence underlying the mestizo's existence is a hidden violence, a violence at the root of all segregation. The empire's law outlaws marriages, fraternizing, even just living together. Its order and the ambitions of its project come at this price. Moreover, the law relegates the mestizo, fruit of these unions, to nonexistence. He must necessarily be on one side or the other, either white or colored. There are no intermediate categories. Here the empire reaches its intimate contradiction, the one signing its death warrant. In order to exist, the empire must reject what was the initial reason for its project. It destroys its own flesh.

Destroys it, rather than recognizing it. For the empire, enclosing each person within the limits of their own ethnic community is a manner of self-destruction. Desire is forced to echo its own image. It sees its own reflection, like Narcissus. What's lacking is precisely what was the Empire's initial project: the encounter with the other and the interlacing of desires. The unavowed postulate of all ethnocentrisms: it is in a mirror-image of myself that I can recognize myself, it is with people who resemble me that self-realization can be achieved. That historically, and even for long periods, peace was obtained in this manner cannot be denied. But at what price? The price of institutional violence, of daily repression. The Empire has no other means of action. And one day, the mestizos, the ignored, the rejected will seize power. Just as with the metics and the barbarians in antiquity, the mestizos of Latin America, with the revolutions at the beginning of the nineteenth century, will become the decisive force overthrowing the Spanish Empire.

We can consequently easily understand that the mestizo is considered a dangerous being in most societies. What's to be done with him? What place to assign him? Categorizing him is impossible. But history unites differences, history is mestizo, history goes forward only through *mestizaje*. As Octavio Paz says, "The labyrinth of the Mestizo is the labyrinth of all men."[15]

Notes

1. Gustave DROYSEN, *Alexandre le Grand,* Paris, Editions Complexe, 1991 (translated from German). There is a considerable bibliography on Alexander. We've used the present text, first published in 1833, because the modern "myth" of Alexander arguably finds in it one of its most significant expressions. Cf., *Encyclopaedia Universalis,* article "Droysen," Johann Gustav (1808–1884).

2. Gustave DROYSEN, op. cit., pg. 443:

Dans le flame de son desir, Alexandre fit apporter le pain selon la coutume chez lui. C'etait la chez les macedoniens, le symbole le plus sacre de l'union charnelle. On le partageait avec une epee et chaque epoux y goutait. De la sorte, le roi de l'Asie et de l'Eurp[e s'unit en marriage a une captive qui allair lui donner l'enfant qui commanderait aux vainqueers.

3. In Oliver REVERDIN, *Alexandre le Grand, image et realite entretiens sur l'Antiquite classique,* T. XXII, Geneva, 1976, pg. 161.

4. Oliver REVERDIN, op. cit., Preface.

5. Tzvetan TODOROV, *Le Conquete de l'Amerique,* Paris, Seuil, 1982, pg. 12.

6. The text can be found in Miguel LEON-PORTILLA, *La filosofia Nahuati,* Mexico, 1959, pg. 129–31. Cf. Jean Marie Gustave LE CLEZIO, *Le reve mexicain, ou la pensee interrompue,* Paris, Gallimard, 1988.

7. Hernan Cortez, *Le Conquete du Mexique,* Paris, Francios Maspero, La Decouverte, First letter, pg. 5:

Le Cacique de Tabasco lui offrit vingt Indiennes. Parmi ces dernieres s'en trouvait une de condition noble fort bien faite et d'une beaute qui pouvait passer pour rare . . . elle fut beptisee quelque temos après sous le nom de Marint. . . . Elle parlait les langues et expliquait aux Indiens dans celle du Mexique et expliquait a Aguiliar dans celle de Yucatan, Cortes etant oblige d;attendre que ses paroles eussent fait ce tour, jusqu'a cr que Maring eut appris le castillian.

8. Cf. Carhage, *L'histoire, sa trace et son echo,* catalogue of the exhibit held at the Petit Palais, Paris-Musees, 1995.

9. Cf. op. cit., pg. 235, quote from Aeluis Aristides, second century A.D., disclosure XXVI, 63, 65:

Vous avez fait que le mot "Romain" n'appartienne pas a une cite mais qu'il soit le nom d'une sorte de race collective, et ce n'est pad une race parmi toutes les autres,mais une sorte de contrpoids aux autres. Aujourd'hui, vous ne separaz pas les races entre les Grecs et les barbares, mais vous avez divise les peoples entre romains et no-romains. . . . Pourtant, l'envie ne regne pas dans votre empire. Car vous avez ete vous-memes les premiers a ne pas donner avec mauvaise grace, puisque vous avez tout mis a la disposition de tous et tout octroye a ceux qui sont capables de ne pas etre des sujets mais des maitres.

10. Cf. Alain BADIOU, *Saint Paul, Le fondation de l'universalisme*, Paris, PUF, 1973.

11. Octavio PAZ, *Le labyrinth de la solitude*, Paris, Gallimard, 1972 (translated from Spanish), pg. 81:

Le symbole de la dechirure est done Malinche, la maitresse indienne de Cortes. Il est vrai qu'elle s'est donnee volotairement au conquistadoe, mais celui-ci des qu'elle cessa de lui etre utile, l'oublia. Dona Marina, pour lui donner son nom chretien s'est convertie en une figure qui represente les Indiennes, fascines, violees ou seduites par les Espangnols.

12. In the *New York Times*, March 26, 1997.

13. Octavio PAZ, *Sor Juana Ines de la Cruz* (translated from Spanish), NRF, Paris, Gallimard, 1987, pg. 53:

Le metis etait l'image vivante de l'illegitimite. Du sentiment d'illegitimite venair son insecurite, son instability perpetuelle, ses allees et venues d'une extreme a l'autre, du courage a al panique, de l'exaltation a l'apathiem de la loyaute a la trahison. . . . Dans une soriete ou le division du travail coincidiat plus strictement qu'en d'autres avec les hierarchies socials, le metis etait litteralement un homme sans postion.

14. Hernan Cortez, op. cit., Letter 4, pg. 236.

15. Octavio PAZ, *Le labyrinth de la solitude*, op. cit., pg 145.

CHAPTER SIX

~

Democracy: Rupture and Turning Point

How does one categorize and characterize *mestizaje*? Even the reflection concerning *mestizaje* remains in history's margins. No wonder. Marked by violence in the traditional empires, the reality per se of *mestizaje* is allowed no role in the thought and reflection around modernity. Modern political theories are built precisely by excluding the particularisms that constitute *mestizaje*. These theories only take shape by positing universal categories as a principle for understanding societies: power, economy, social classes, which reject outside their limits what *mestizaje* highlights. The inequalities and the violence of *mestizaje* will at most be seen as circumstantial elements, which can be reduced to and explained by general mechanisms that transcend them. "Racial" conflicts, irritating because recurrent, will be explained in terms of economic conflicts or power struggles. And if a Mestizo group's specificity is given recognition, this specificity can only be temporary, local, and destined to disappear in the larger current of history. *Mestizaje* is thus emptied of what is uniquely its own: its position (bespoken by physical features) transgressing, in any given society, the assigned, clearly identified roles.

Add to this that even though a few authors attempted to give more breadth to the reflection on *mestizaje*, they never achieved the status of reference works. Above all, their conceptual tools proved incapable of validating *mestizaje* as an object of analysis. Its diversity is impossible to

78

reduce to unity. There are different forms of *mestizaje* and multiple experiences of encounters between different peoples. Can a theory of *mestizaje* be elaborated? Unfortunately for us, Gobineau, the only person seriously to have tried, made it an instrument of discrimination. What's more, *mestizaje* seems to resist analysis, for as Francois Laplantine and Alexis Nouss remark: "Mestizaje is not strictly speaking «something»."[1] Once again, whether from a theoretical or a practical point of view, *mestizaje* slips through our fingers.

Tenacious, however, *mestizaje* isn't that easy to exclude from the social field. It took not only the third world's entrance on the scene but also the transformation of Western societies through immigration before the questions contained in *mestizaje* began being formulated in terms of their specificity. So rather than reducing it to the well-worn theories of social analysis, it's worth making a fresh effort to try to delineate it. But first of all, let us try to understand why the attempts of the past were useless and why they failed.

Mestizaje Doesn't Exist: Cornelius de Pauw

For Cornelius de Pauw (1739–1799) *mestizaje* doesn't exist. He nevertheless writes a book about it whose aim is to demonstrate that *mestizaje* is fated to disappear. In his book, *Recherches philosophiques sur les Amérindiens, mémoire intéressant pour server l'histoire de l'espèce humaine* (Philosophical research on the Amerindians, an interesting treatise to further the history of the human species), published in Berlin in 1774, de Pauw sets forth a theory of human *mestizaje*.[2] He has never traveled to the New World but has accumulated information and extensive documentation on the new populations. He draws a portrait of these "savages": "natural" men, untouched by history, degenerates, apathetic, sexually rather inactive, ultimately unsalvageable, in short, an inferior race.

De Pauw's objective is to demonstrate that the fruit of union between Europeans and Indians is not fated to last. He charts the different kinds of *mestizaje*, using the well-known vocabulary—quadroons, octoroons—in order to show that after five generations, *mestizaje* disappears and the dominant race completely recovers its purity. On the time line of generations, *mestizaje* is a temporary accident. Only the main races remain, identical to how the Creator originally made them.

No trace in de Pauw of the ideas of stage, history, education, even though they were beginning to appear among his contemporaries. His is a static world, immutably established from its inception. This kind of world makes no room for *mestizaje*.

De Pauw is not a major author. He reflects more a way of thinking than he actually influences his period. But it's interesting to note, as Michel Lalonde observes, that popular French discourse on genetics today coincides with de Pauw's discourse on genetics. "The two systems drive at the same conclusion, the non-existence of a durable filiation rooted in Mestizaje, through a genetic annulment kept alive two centuries later by a linguistic silence."[3]

In short, de Pauw simply gives form to and tries to justify the stereotypes mentioned in the beginning of this book: only major races exist and they are the reference point for everything. The mestizo is an exception. It's impossible to define him and to speak about him except by referring to the original races having produced him. He is an exotic anecdote. This is true in the eyes of the others as well as in his own eyes, the mestizo often aspiring to just melt into the crowd of his "fellows." Need it be said, this is how the mestizo is regarded often in the eyes of numerous scholars and intellectuals who, except for Roger Bastide or Octavio Paz, were unable to comprehend the mestizo except through categories that negated him.

It's true that the sole attempt to put forward a broad theory of *mestizaje* in relation to societies and cultures ended with consequences so disastrous that it remains stigmatized with infamy in intellectual history. But isn't it true that Gobineau, for we are referring to him, by making *mestizaje* a universal key ends up, like others, denying its specificity?

Inegalitarian *Mestizaje*: Arthur de Gobineau

Gobineau (1816–1882) intends to explain social diversity using a unique explanatory principle. This principle is *mestizaje*, which he calls "ethnic mix." "One of the key ideas of this essay, is the important influence of ethnic mixes, i.e. of marriages between different races."[4]

The first two volumes of *Essai sur l'inégalité des races humaines* (Essay concerning the inequality of the human races) by Count Arthur de

Gobineau are published in early summer 1853. With the very first words of his essay, Gobineau indicates his subject: "The collapse of civilizations is the most striking and the most obscure of history's phenomena."[5]

Right from the start, Gobineau considers human diversity a result of decadence. He is interested in studying the collapse of civilizations, a phenomenon posited as self-evident, the way he posits as equally self-evident the explanation for this collapse:

> It was necessary that I fully absorb the self-evident idea that the ethnic question dominates all of history's other problems, holds their key, and that the inequality between the races forming a nation is sufficient to explain how the destinies of peoples unfold.[6]

From the outset, two postulates are thus affirmed: the postulate of the fall of civilizations as a phenomenon to explain, and the postulate of *mestizaje* as the explanatory principle. His aim: explain the diversity in history's forms, that is, the multiple types of societies and civilizations. In order to achieve his aim, he holds one point of view: the ethnic group one belongs to; and one object for analysis: the factor of racial inequality. This inequality due to *mestizaje* is for him instrumental in causing the differentiation of human groups and, he adds, human degeneration.

His essay develops these affirmations. Humanity is degenerating, and this cannot be explained by the state of institutions, by moral decay, or by human actions, but by one factor and one factor only: ethnic differences. There begins a process of intermixing, beginning with one unique family enshrining "all that is great, noble and fertile on this Earth . . . the 'Aryan' family . . . white," that leads to inequalities and to the degeneration of civilizations. This is the objective of Gobineau's *synthesis* which he expects will revolutionize the intellectual world and the science of mankind.

Observer, voyager, author, Gobineau's goal is explaining, illustrating, and proving this hypothesis. By trying to uncover a unique principle explaining the multitude of forms taken by social bonds over time and enabling their evaluation, Gobineau is part of the school of global theories of history.[7] He has a dual preoccupation: that his approach be scientific (he regularly affirms this), meaning that it aim at elaborating a theory based on facts, and that his approach be normative, meaning that it indicate an orientation for collective behavior, that is, politics.

In his view, the two, science and politics (action), are united in the concept of *degenerescence*, a degenerescence linked to the pureness of blood altered by admixtures. According to him, human societies are characterized by the process of degeneration they are experiencing. This process is linked to the pureness of blood, of which mankind and civilization are a product. The sequence goes something like this: ethnic mixing, impurity of blood, degeneration of individuals, decadence of societies.

> I consequently believe that the word "degenerate" as applied to a people, must and does signify that this people no longer has the intrinsic value they formerly did, because they no longer have the same blood in their veins, since a series of succeeding combinations has modified its value; in other words, although the name is still the same, this people has not preserved the same race as its founders; lastly that man in this state of decadence, the man we call degenerate, is a different product, from the ethnic point of view, than the heroes of the grand eras.[8]

At the beginning of humanity there existed, according to Gobineau, a pure race, possessing, thanks to this purity, all the attributes of civilization, a race that could be considered superior. It was the white race, and it was at the inception of all the great human civilizations. The process of *mestizaje*, or racial mixing, allows the other civilizations to benefit from the qualities of the white race, but this mixing represents a process of degeneration for humanity.

Thus for Gobineau, biological makeup determines the whole of human relations. Biological differences ground social inequalities. Tocqueville will tell him: "You reduce everything to the biological." Reducing the social and the cultural to the biological is embarking upon a road not only mistaken but dangerous, because it dehumanizes human beings. As Levi-Strauss writes:

> Anthropology's original sin lies in the confusion between the biological notion of race (supposing this notion can claim to be objective even in the limited field, something which modern genetics contests) and the sociological and psychological productions of human cultures. Once Gobineau committed this original sin, he found himself trapped in the infernal circle that leads from an intellectual error not excluding good faith to the involuntary validation of all attempts at discrimination and oppression.[9]

Gobineau is not small-minded, but he is wrong-minded. He is part of the movement running through the nineteenth century that tries to find a scientific explanation for the human condition. But he embarks up a dead-end street. Unfortunately, he had followers who were responsible for some of the worst excesses of the twentieth century. Nazism and apartheid claimed his ideas, and it's not certain that this posterity has entirely disappeared. This posterity is recurrent, and for order's sake, it wants to recognize the mestizo, but only partially and unequally, since the weak, in sharing their blood, share some qualities of the strong. Analyses of this kind will reinforce and legitimate all kinds of exclusions. There is no such thing as inegalitarian recognition. Tocqueville will never cease repeating this to Gobineau.

Liberty Protests: Alexis de Tocqueville

In October 1853, Tocqueville (1805–1859) received the first two volumes of Gobineau's *Essay* which came out at the beginning of summer.[10] The two men had known each other for a long time, since the end of 1842 or early 1843. They had a friendship that was full of deference and gratitude on Gobineau's part for his elder of eleven years who had helped him with his career, and on Tocqueville's part, he was faithful and efficient, for he esteemed the ambitious young man he had made the chief of his staff during his stint as foreign minister in the Second Republic. Their relationship had already revolved around questions of social ethics since Tocqueville, member of the Academy, had requested the young Gobineau to read and summarize for him various texts on the history of moral science as well as to prepare summaries on different European authors.[11] They had therefore already exchanged and confronted their views on these questions. But the publication of the *Essay* crystallized their clash.

For the next six years, until Tocqueville's death in 1859, they continued exchanging letters concerning Gobineau's ideas. Of the eighty-one letters today forming their correspondence, seventeen deal directly with Gobineau's *Essay* and what Tocqueville calls his *system*. The last two volumes of the *Essay* were published in the spring of 1855, when Gobineau was on his way to Teheran as France's representative. These volumes aggravated the differences between them. Their friendship reached the breaking point because their assumptions, their arguments, and their conclusions about human identity and the future of societies diverged so broadly. In these letters we find two clashing conceptions of the social bond and, consequently, of the underpinnings of the ethics of life in society.[12]

Six days after receiving the books, Tocqueville answered Gobineau. He expressed his opposition straight away and almost instinctively:

> I've never hidden from you my great prejudice against your core idea; I confess this idea seems to me to belong to the family of materialistic theories and even to be one of its most dangerous members, since a fatality deriving from constitution is no longer merely applied to the individual but to these collections of individuals called races and which are still alive.[13]

"Materialism, fatality, the worst of all hypotheses, false and pernicious doctrines," in letter after letter the adjectives express Tocqueville's embarrassment and disagreement. Something in him puts up a resistance to Gobineau's reasoning and he even admits how torn he is between the esteem he feels for him and the repulsion his ideas inspire in him: "I'm ceaselessly divided over this work. I disapprove of the book and like its author."[14]

What are Tocqueville's objections to what Gobineau writes? To begin with, the materialistic nature of his thinking, since he wants to explain humanity's state only using elements of a material nature and first and foremost, a person's *biological constitution*. Gobineau rejects the word *materialist*, because he considers himself a Christian. Tocqueville, although not convinced, won't press the point but will express himself more precisely. By materialistic, he means deterministic. The destiny of mankind depends on the fatality of material elements, making the notion of liberty irrelevant. Explaining and judging human beings, individuals and groups, according to their ethnic group, or to use Gobineau's words, their *biological constitution*; isn't this denying them what belongs uniquely to humanity? Human society depends on something else, something that takes precedence over biology. For Tocqueville, this something is called liberty.

What's more, Gobineau claims to have developed a system, in other words a global explanation. For him, racial inequality, the degeneration of races from supposedly pure origins, and their intermixing through *mestizaje* are capable of furnishing an explanation for the inequality of all civilizations as well as for humanity's irreversible decadence. Tocqueville, not without malice, remarks that such a pretension is impossible because by definition the future escapes us. It's not possible to speak of science in relation to a largely unknown object. Consequently, it's pretentious for Gobineau to believe that his system can make the human sciences progress. And although Gobineau says how very sad Tocqueville's position makes him, the latter will never agree with the alleged scientific nature of the former's arguments.

He never will because Gobineau's fatalism—fatalism of constitution, of race—leaves no room for approximation. Tocqueville compares it to predestination of the most rigorous kind. He evokes Jansenism and Calvinism, the two most rigorous theological doctrines regarding the fatality imprisoning human freedom, and even writes that in his eyes, there is hardly any difference between this theological fatalism and Gobineau's materialistic fatalism. Both kinds argue that human beings are the objects of absolute constraint and necessity. In both cases, it's human beings who lose out.

> Your doctrine is a kind of fatalism, or predestination if you will, different from Saint Augustine's, the Jansenists' and the Calvinists' (they resemble you the most because of doctrinal absoluteness) insofar as with you, there is a very strong link between predestination and matter. Thus you continuously speak of races that regenerate themselves or deteriorate, that acquire or lose social capacities they didn't have, through an "infusion of different blood," I think these are your very expressions. This kind of predestination seems to me to be a pure materialism.[15]

In considering that human beings are determined by biological *with* social mechanisms, we wind up with alienation and destruction of the human being. This thinking discloses a deep contempt, a betrayal of humankind, and Tocqueville does not use gloves when writing this to his correspondent: "You have no love for humanity. . . ."

Along with these more intellectual arguments, Tocqueville also sets out practical ones. Gobineau's doctrine can only have the worst consequences for humanity. It's a disaster for individuals and societies. He lists its effects: *contempt, apathy, violence* . . . in one word, it deprives humans of what makes them human: their liberty, their free will. "This results in human liberty being greatly restricted, if not completely abolished."

> If at least your doctrine were useful for humanity. . . . But it's clearly just the opposite. What advantage can there possibly be in persuading a group of people, cowardly, living in barbarity, in indolence or in servitude, that there is nothing to be done to improve their condition, change their morals or modify their government, since they are the way they are because of the nature of their race? Don't you see that your doctrine naturally leads to all the ills that permanent inequality engenders: pride, violence, contempt for one's fellowmen, tyranny and abjection in all its forms?[16]

The aristocrat, friend, and evangel of a democracy adopted with mind and heart puts his finger on the sore spot of his correspondent's intellectual edifice. For Gobineau, race and biology rule everything. From such a system flows Gobineau's stance that human groups must be ruled by violence, the stronger dominating the weaker. For him, this is not just a fact but a right, and we now know what monstrous aberrations result from this way of thinking.

Tocqueville immediately sees the danger: an unleashing of violence and contempt. For him, humanity is perfectible, and education is the indispensable tool if humanity is to progress. Although humanity may be a disappointment, it can be educated: it's the sole way, or there will be no more humanity. Tocqueville, the aristocrat who now and then misses the Ancien Régime, concedes that in former times perhaps the use of force was more efficient. But Tocqueville, the democrat-by-choice, immediately affirms the preeminence of liberty over any other consideration:

> In my eyes what makes human societies, as well as individuals, what they are is the exercise of their liberty. That liberty is harder to establish and maintain in certain of our democratic societies than in certain of the earlier aristocratic societies, this is something I have always said. But that it be impossible, I will never be foolhardy enough to think it. That we should despair of ever succeeding, I pray God that he never inspires me with the idea. No, I will never believe that this human species at the head of all visible creation has become this bastardized flock you tell us it is, and that there is no choice but to hand it over, without any future and any recourse, to a small number of shepherds who, in the end, are not better animals than we, and often are worse.[17]

The issue here concerns an attitude toward humanity, a choice between contempt and lucid, sincere love.

It also concerns a choice about religion. Or to be more exact, their debate illustrates two attitudes about Christianity as a civilizing factor. In their previous correspondence over morality, Gobineau and Tocqueville had already clashed. And at one point Tocqueville cannot refrain from pointing out how Gobineau's system, since it leads to violence, moves away from Christian tradition.

> You must recognize that although you pay lip-service to the Church and that you deploy enormous efforts, perhaps in good faith, in order to not take a position outside the Church's bosom, the core of your system is hostile to the Church, and all of the consequences we can legitimately infer from your system are more or less in contradiction with the Church's ideas.[18]

Gobineau responds with sharp pique: "No, if I say I'm Catholic, then I am!" Tocqueville in his next letter comes back to this, but six months have gone by and the two correspondents are now far apart, one in France and the other in Central Asia:

> You took to heart I don't know what flip remark I made about your religion. This proves that one should not tease friends who are two or three deserts and as many seas distant, since an aggravating word can only be soothed a year later.

Then Tocqueville proceeds to set out all the points of disagreement between Gobineau's doctrine and the Church's traditions. On the subject of the unity of the human species and of monogenism that Gobineau calls into question, and especially on the equality between men, he writes:

> Christianity obviously attempted to make all men brothers and equal. Your doctrine makes them cousins at most, whose common father is only in heaven. There are only victors and vanquished, masters and slaves, by virtue of their birth.[19]

We are at the heart of a paradox: of these two men, the one who explicitly refers to Christianity and vehemently protests that he is Christian, is in fact the one radically opposed to the evangelical message. And the one who apparently never ceased to doubt, or at least never claimed to be a believer,[20] perhaps out of extreme modesty, is the one who recognizes in the Gospel and the Church the forces elevating humans, consecrating their liberty and guaranteeing equality between them. A paradox in appearance only, once more illustrating the permanent, underlying presence of different models of Church-society relations as they resulted from the French Revolution.

Tocqueville's criticism of Gobineau compels us to go to the very foundations of racist thought. Neither one of them of course used the word *racism* since it won't be coined before the beginning of the twentieth century. But although the word is never uttered, the object is clearly at the heart of their debate. It is a debate between two demanding minds for whom politeness of form and elegant language in no way diminish exactness of thought and frankness of expression. Gobineau illustrates the implacable logic of fatalist thinking which, because it postulates inequality, can only lead to violence and ultimately to the destruction of what is specifically human. Opposing him, Tocqueville affirms that humanity is responsible for its destiny, which only liberty and equality can shape.

It's an ethical debate too whose anthropological corollaries are apparent in the *Correspondence*. Among these corollaries are the inanity and the noxiousness of an ethical system claiming a basis in biological fact. For Tocqueville, the nature of man is not a function of biological determinism but of liberty and free will. This is what makes individuals, as well as society, human. A few months before his death, Tocqueville, in the last letter on the subject, shares the following observation with Gobineau.

> I feel great attachment for you as well as esteem and affection. But between the temperaments of our two souls, there are differences and even clashes that produce what you justly bemoan. I love mankind; I find it very agreeable to be able to esteem its members, and I know of nothing sweeter than the feeling of admiration when it's possible. . . . As for you, perhaps it's your nature, perhaps it's the consequences of the unpleasant battles you courageously fought as a young man, you have become used to feeding on the contempt humanity in general, and your country in particular, inspire in you.[21]

It is a strange destiny of an intellectual friendship, initiated in close collaboration and ending in an acknowledgment of totally contradictory views of the world and of action. "In conclusion and with your permission, I wish to stop discussing your political theories," writes Tocqueville.

Democracy is not reduced to silence along with him. In the face of the inescapable and universal phenomenon of the encounter between human beings and of *mestizaje*, which Gobineau's systematic postulates helped more to discredit than to explicate, democracy must take up Tocqueville's arguments and his positions. These positions leave no room for ambiguity of any kind. Being opposed to racism is not just a question of good will, or even a moral question in the strict sense; it's opting for a vision of humanity. It's about knowing what kind of humanity we envision and what kind of society we want to build.

Democracy is the passage from tribe to citizen status. Its aims are equality and universalism. With democracy, a new conception of human identity as applicable to everyone, thus universal, and offering equal recognition for all individuals appears. Consequently, there is no middle ground between democracy and tribal society. Reconciling Gobineau and Tocqueville is impossible. It's true—as Tocqueville himself remarks—that democracy can take an inegalitarian, even a totalitarian, form. It can betray its ideals, in fact. The same Tocqueville, regarding the question of the colonies, will hesitate about the pertinent stand to take. Nonetheless, he considers education the way to advance along the road to an inevitable democracy, even if in certain cases he thinks its advent seems a long way off. The dream of empire is henceforward defunct. Nostalgia for Alexander and the past is replaced by a forward-looking project of a democratic society which, through a kind of ripple effect, will spread to the entire planet.

In the space thus opened, the mestizo has a place. Not the place de Pauw or Gobineau assign him or her. Both of them put *mestizaje* in the category of "natural" phenomena, whether this nature, as for de Pauw, is immutably fixed since its origins or whether, as for Gobineau, nature's forms change over time. But *mestizaje*, as Bastide reminds us, concerns social races. There's a connection between *mestizaje* and society, consequently making it a social and cultural phenomenon, that is a human phenomenon. The recognition of differences, the encounters between people, the transcending of violence are henceforward at the initiative of citizens. The sense and meaning of *mestizaje* change, and it's with this change in mind that we must try to comprehend it and determine its place in our modern democracies.

Notes

1. Francois LAPLANTINE, Alexis NOUSS, op. cit., pg. 82.

2. Cornelius de PAUW, *Recherches philosophiques sur les amérindiens*, Preface by Michel Duchet, 2 volumes, Paris, J. M. Place, 1991.

3. Michel LALONDE, *Métissage et texte Beur*, in Bernard HUE, op. cit., p. 108.

4. Arthur de GOBINEAU, *Essai sur l'inégalité des races humaines*, Dedication in the first edition.

5. Arthur de GOBINEAU, op. cit., chapter 1, *Oeuvres complètes*, Bibliothèque de la Pléiade, 3 volumes, Paris, Gallimard, 1983, vol. 1, pg. 141.

6. Arthur de GOBINEAU, Dedication in the first edition, *A sa mejesté Georges V, roi de Hanovre*, op. cit., pg. 138:

> J'ai dû me pénétrer de cette évidence que la quesiton ethnique domine tous les autres problèmes de l'historire, en tient la clef, et que l'inégalité des races dont le concours forme une nation, suffit à expliquer tout l'enchaînement des destinées des peuples.

7. On racial theories and Gobineau's predecessors, Michel FOUCAULT makes interesting reading. *Il faut défendre la société*, Cours au Collège de France, 1976, Paris, Gallimard-Seuil, 1997.

8. GOBINEAU, op. cit., chapter 4:

> Je pense donc que le mot dégénéré s'appliquant à un peuple, doit signifier et signifie que ce peuple n'a plus la valeur intrinsèque qu'autrefois il possédait, parce qu'il n'a plus dans les veines le même sang, dont les alliages successifs ont graduellement modifié la valeur; autrement dit qu'avec le même nom, il n'a pas conservé la même race que ses fondateurs; enfin que l'homme de la décadence, celui qu'on appelle l'homme dégénéré, est un produit différent, du point de vue ethnique, du héros des grandes éposques.

9. Claude LEVI-STRAUSS, *Anthropologie structurale deux*, Paris, Plon, 1973, pg. 378:

> Le péché originel de l'Anthropologie consiste dans la confusion entre la notion biologique de race (à supposer que même sur le terrain limité, cette notion puisse prétendre à l'objectivité, ce que la génétique moderne conteste) et les production sociologiques of psychologiques des cultures humaines. Il a suffi à Gobineau de l'avoir commis pour se trouver enfermé dans le cercle infernal qui conduct d'une erreur intellectuelle n'excluant pas la bonne foi, à la légitimation involontaire de toutes les tentatives de discrimination et d'oppression.

10. On relations between Tocqueville and Gobineau, see the volume containing their correspondence in *Correspondence d'Alexis de Tocqueville et d'Arthur de*

Gobineau, Alexis de TOCQUEVILLE, Oeuvres complètes, Tome IX, text established and annotated by M. Degros, Introduction by J. J. Chevallier, Foreword by J. P. Mayer, Paris, Gallimard, 1959.

11. The first letters they exchange are about this work and the notes referred to can be found at the end of the volume *Correspondence.*

12. On the evolution in the respective positions of the two correspondents, the excellent Introduction by J. J. Chevallier makes for very interesting reading, op. cit., pg. 9–35. It's not our intention to retrace this evolution but simply to highlight each protagonist's presuppositions.

13. Letter of October 11, 1853, op. cit., num. 47, pg. 199:

> Je ne voius ai jamais caché que j'avais un grand préjugé contre votre idée mère, laquelle me semble, je l'avoue appartenir à la famille des théories matérialistes et en être même un des plus dangereux membres, puisque c'est la fatalité de la constitution appliquée, non plus à l'individu seulement, mais à ces collections d'individus qu'on nomme races et qui vivent toujours.

14. Letter of January 8, 1856, op. cit., num. 66, pg. 245.

15. Letter of November 17, 1853, op. cit., num. 48, pg. 202:

> Votre doctrine est une sorte de fatalisme, de prédestination si vous voulez, différente de celle de Saint Augustin, des jansénistes et des Calvinistes (ce sont eux qui vous ressemblent le plus par l'absolu de la doctrine) en ce qu'il y a chez vous un lien très étroit entre le fait de la prédestination et la matière. Ainsi vous parlez sans cesse de races qui se régénèrent ou se détériorent, qui prenent ou quittent des capacités sociales qu'elles n'avaient pas par une "infusion d sang différent," je crois que ce sont vos propres expressions. Cette prédestination-là me paraît, je vous l'avouerai, du pur matérialisme.

16. Letter of November 17, 1853, op. cit., num. 48, pg. 203:

> Encore . . . si votre doctrine était utile à l'humanité . . . mais c'est évidemment le contraire, quel intérêt peut-il y avoir à persuader des peuples lâches qui vivent dans la barbarie, dans la mollesse ou dans la servitude, qu'étant tels de par la natur de leur race, if n'y a a rien à faire pour améliorer leur condition, changer leurs moeurs ou modifier leur gouvernement? Ne voyez-vous pas que de votre doctrine sortent naturellement tous les maux que l'inégalité permanente enfante: l'orgueil, la violence, le mépris du semblable, la tyrannie et l'abjection sous toutes ses formes.

17. Letter of January 24, 1875, op. cit., num. 72, pg. 280:

> A mes yeux, les sociétés humaines comme les individus ne sont quelque chose que par l'usage de leur liberté. Que la liberté soit plus difficile à fonder et à maintenir

dans certaines sociétés démocratiques comme les nôtres que dans certaines sociétés aristocratiques qui nous ont précédés, je l'ai toujours dit. Mais que cela soit impossible, aristocratiques qui nous ont precedes, je l'ai toujours dit. Mais que cela soit impossible, je ne seral jamais assez téméraire pour le penser. Qu'il faille désespérer d'y réussir, je prie Dieu de no jamais m'en inspirer l'idée. Non, je ne croirai point que cette espèce humaine qui est a la tete de la creation visible soit devenue ce troupeau abatardi que humaine qui est à la tête de la création visible soit devenue ce troupeau abâtardi que vous nous dites, et qu'il n'y ait plus qu'à la livrer sans avenir et sans ressource à un petit nombre de bergers qui après tout ne sont pas de meilleur animaux que nous et souvent en sont de pires.

18. Letter of July 30, 1856, op. cit., num. 70, pg. 265:

Il faut bien reconnaitre que, bien que vous donniez des coups de chapeau à l'Eglise, et que vous fassiez peut-être de conne foi, de grands efforts pour ne pas vous placer hors de son giron, le fond même de votre système lui est hostlie et que presque toutes les conséquences qu'on est en droit d'en tirer vont plus ou moins contre ses propres idées.

19. Letter of January 24, 1857, op. cit., num. 72, pg. 277:

Le christianisme a évidemment tendu à faire de tous les hommes des frères et des égaux. Votre doctrine n'en fait tout au plus que des cousins dont le père commun n'est qu'au ciel. Il n'y a que des vainqueurs et des vaincus, des maîtres et des esclaves par droit de naissance.

20. Cf. Alexis de TOCQUEVILLE, Letter to Madame Swetchine dated February 6, 1857, op. cit., vol. XV, pg. 313: "Until then my life had unfolded surrounded by faith. . . . Then doubt entered my soul."

21. Letter of September 16, 1858, op. cit., num. 78, pg. 296:

Je vous suis très attaché, j'ai de l'estime et de l'affection pur vous. Mais if y a entre les tempéraments de nos deux âmes des différences et même des contrariétés qui produisent ce dont vous vous plaigenez, non à tort. J'aime les hommes; ce m'est très agréable de pouvoir les estimer et je ne connais rien de plus doux que le sentiment de l'admiration quand if est possible. . . . Quant à vous, soit naturel, soit conséquences des luttes pénibles auxquelles votre jeunesse s'est courageusement livrée, vous vous êtes habitué à vivre du mépris que vous inspire l'humanité en général et en particulier votre pays.

CHAPTER SEVEN

~

The Transformation of Bonds

Democracy creates a special bond called citizenship. The democratic state is not the Empire. It's not imposed against the people's will but results from the social contract among the members of society. They empower the democratic state and exercise control over it. The vote is the expression of this contract and the instrument of control. The democratic bond consequently creates a new "space," different in nature from the other zones in society, thus making it necessary to review them. Polity articulated with civil society and economy are the "three-legged stool" that Hillary Clinton sees as the key element in the attempt to "civilize democracy."[1]

From this perspective, the word "*mestizaje*" takes on a different signification. From negative, it becomes positive. The word is broadening its field and increasingly designates the cultural dimension of the encounter between peoples. True, it still remains a slippery word. Depending on groups and contexts, it can be understood differently, and we must be careful each time to precisely define its scope. But on the social plane, it's a kind of "revealing acid." Acceptance of *mestizaje* or interest for what it represents reveals how open a society is to democracy. Therefore, we must attempt to define *mestizaje*'s place in contemporary society.

Naturally, *mestizaje* did not disappear along with empires, but in the context of democratic societies, it designates new forms of living together. It no longer indicates a biological determinism (which for a long time fueled phantasms and was exploited by empires in establishing order) but a certain type of societal relations. Democracy forces into broad daylight what the word *mestizaje* dissimulated and which constituted its ambiguity. It was a word used to indicate difference and by the same token transform this difference into inequality. That's why in most societies it provoked discrimination and connoted exclusion. Acceding to democracy means a 180-degree turn from this way of perceiving things. For democracy, *mestizaje* still designates difference. However, this difference no longer leads to discrimination; it invites mutual recognition.

Democracy is definitely not about erasing human differences. No societies, except those of apartheid, can claim to suppress diversity, whether it be ethnic differences or differences in origins, education, or culture. The recognition and the valuation of this diversity represent, for contemporary societies, one of their most important riches and attract people from all over the planet to these societies. This recognition represents the inevitable stakes at risk for democracies. It becomes one of the major tasks facing democratic societies.

Mestizaje, insofar as it points out differences and the way they intermix, becomes the best locus for this recognition to operate. *Mestizaje* puts some "slack" into ethnic ties. How then to deal with the new relations being shaped between democratic identity and the different cultures with their particularisms? How does democracy transform the relationship between cultures and allow their recognition?

Shifting Boundaries

The first thing indicating that something is new is the fluidity of borders, often perceived at first in a negative way. One of the distinctive traits of multiculturalism is precisely that borders no longer seem as secure. The fantasy image of a country protected by its borders and corresponding to one "race" and one culture is replaced by the feeling that borders have become porous and ultimately impossible to pin down. First of all, this means geographical borders, which movements in populations seem easily to ignore, but it also means the frontiers of information, the borders of ideals and values. As geography becomes less circumscribed, culture and ethics go more out of focus. This way of thinking provides the basis for the Cassandra speeches against the opening-up of borders, accepting foreigners, and becoming more world-oriented. This nourishes negativity, invoking in turn the risk of a loss of identity and the threat of new barbarian invasions. In this view, *mestizaje* is total subversion, radical treason, allowing the foreigner in. The mestizo becomes the Trojan Horse of the West's destruction. This view makes the North Atlantic world a fortress and forgets the last five centuries of its history, which saw an expansion leading to the current globalization. More importantly, it is avoiding, by agitating old fears, what is required by today's global communication. In the name of an alleged homogeneity, whose illusory character we've seen, it is refusing to deal with the differences making up humanity.

From time immemorial managing differences has meant creating borders. Borders separate, borders differentiate. The most visible, at least in our age of modern nations, are the geographical borders. The lines they trace are indicated by posts and guarded by armies, thus determining an inside and an outside. Inside, we have our fellow citizens. Outside are the foreigners. Along with this geographical frontier come all the elements that for our countries form national identity: lifestyle and symbols that differentiate and by the same token separate human beings into different groups. And need we add, into long-standing enemies. Crossing a border requires procedures that vary with time and transportation means as well as politics. Some borders are closed and practically impossible to cross, others are open and continue opening up. Thanks to borders, the planet is not some undifferentiated space. The way the earth has been inhabited over time has crisscrossed it with lines animated by the colors and names of our geography schoolbooks. Cultural borders, at least so it's thought, often follow geographical and national borders. The lines on the ground have determined history and in numerous cases still decide peace or war, that is, the destiny of peoples.

Today, and this is really what is new, these lines on the ground, for which so many lives have been sacrificed, seem to be disappearing. They are losing their importance. Necessary on the one hand to avoid indistinctness and to define peoples' identity, they hardly seem to count for much in this age of rapid travel and planetary voyages. They don't show up in satellite photos; proof, if any were needed, that the idea of "natural borders" should be stored with other outdated items. Will the planet be unified and human beings achieve the universal civilization for which some pray? For at the same time that the lines along the ground become more porous, identities have to be redefined. Different peoples enter into contact, intermix, and cultural exchanges are increasing. As a result it's becoming almost impossible now, in the heart of numerous cities, to determine where fashion trends come from, or culinary tastes, or value systems. The stranger/foreigner and the border are everywhere.

But the objection immediately arises: if the border is everywhere, then it's nowhere, not on the ground, not in the mind. Doesn't making borders so uncertain mean dissolving national identity, precisely the very thing that is democracy's strength and base? This fear continuously gives rise to numerous debates. It is why there is so much insistence on the theme of *integration*. Why the national culture is opposed to the other cultures, the indigenous culture opposed to the cultures of the arriving immigrants. Why the old saying, "When in Rome, do as the Romans do," is constantly recalled. Why any contribution from a foreign culture is looked upon askance. And finally, why the fear of barbarians is rekindled, the fear of invasion and destruction of the Empire sleeping at the heart of the West. In this view, cultural *mestizaje* would be the enemy of national identity, a corrosive substance destroying the distinctions that up until now have made it possible to assign identities to human groups.

It is false to see a strong national identity as opposed to cultural *mestizaje*. One does not annul the other. Quite to the contrary, one implies the other. European construction is a good example of the processes at work. A characteristic of this construction is that the national geographic borders are becoming progressively more elastic in order to enable the advent of a new zone, the European zone. However, the advent of this European zone doesn't abolish the specific cultural identity of the various countries. Take the example of language. Since it's vain imagining unifying Europe by imposing a common language, as in the United States, other solutions become necessary, for instance learning another language starting in grade school.

On the other hand, the enlarging of a national "space" into something more vast, the European Community for example, makes us aware of a long-neglected fact: political and cultural borders don't necessarily mesh. This is the crucial point. For a long time these two spaces were expected to coincide. The Empire imposed its culture and the colonial powers their language. Of course, there continued to exist local particularisms which political realism obliged one to respect. But political bonds and cultural identity were expected to mesh, and school was the privileged tool to make this come about.

The identity of individuals living in the same territory was also expected to conform to the common mold, which defined the citizen as someone who spoke the language, contributed to the collective welfare (particularly by serving his country), had access to collective goods, and benefited from the common culture. This was true even if long-opposed particularisms continued existing, like the regional languages in the nineteenth century, and even if a common identity was forged only by paying the price in terms of time and the violence of wars. The nation's ideal remained abolishing particularisms in favor of a citizen identity and a common culture that would absorb all particularisms and be in tune with all the needs of all individuals. It's only recently that, in a country like France, regional differences are encouraged and recognized as legitimate, especially regional languages in the name of Europe. This may seem to be a kind of prudent middle road, and it is. But it's also much more.

Mestizaje appears effectively to challenge the notion that different identities coincide. It doesn't recognize borders; it shifts them, with the result that it is harder for identities to conform to the proposed collective mold. *Mestizaje* makes it necessary to differentiate political borders that can seem to be clearly delineated, a black line on a map; cultural borders are perceived as fuzzy, constantly in flux, impossible to delineate in a lasting way. A cultural border is mobile and runs between people but also runs through each individual. Mestizo children, living witnesses to how mobile cultural borders can be, are also actors in this flux. Through their existence, they are part of two, or even several, cultural groups: those of their parents and grandparents, they are like them, and yet different, "other." They have a double or triple identity, and it's also a new one, as is the case for a fair number of French citizens: Bretons,

Lorraines, Italians, Alsacians, North Africans, and yet they are all fellow citizens of one and the same republic.

Because of the mestizo child, the meaning of borders changes. Borders were a clear-cut line along the ground; also a clear-cut line in people's minds, a line signifying membership in a certain group which in turn determined an identity. An individual was either this or that, French, German, or Italian. Now an individual becomes a citizen possessing multiple memberships. Naturally the line along the ground is still there, as are procedures for crossing it. But henceforward, the outcome of the dialogue now taking shape between politics and culture is not predetermined by the violence of the powers that be.

Mestizaje's long history reveals that even the most protected borders become points of contact and passage. They don't so much illustrate separations between peoples as they do a place where humans meet. Recently a long article in *Newsweek* explained how, despite all the barriers the United States has placed along its border with Mexico, a new culture was taking shape in this border area, the Mexican-American culture.[2] In other words, even if barbed wire runs the length of the Rio Grande, this space to the north of Mexico and to the south of the United States is turning into a new region, increasingly distinct from its neighbors.[3] The border is no longer a line, but a wide ribbon of land. This is a long-familiar phenomenon for old Europe. Political boundaries cut across cultures. In the name of unity, they impose separations. They superpose a new, national identity over the identities whose underpinning are land and region. With the result that in a country like France, its common national identity actually assembles a diversity of regional cultures.[4] The rediscovery and valuation of regional cultures share the same background as the welcoming of the foreign cultures introduced by immigration. Within the same territory, national identity articulates diverse and changing cultural identities. The nation thus becomes a machine for transforming ethnic identities,[5] and multiculturalism's intercultural dialogue, instigated by *mestizaje*, far from destroying democracy, is what fuels it.

Binary or Ternary Dialogue

Taylor's word for describing the relations between cultures in multiculturalism is *dialogic*. "Thus," he writes, "my discovering my own identity doesn't mean that I work it out in isolation, but that I negotiate it through dialogue, partly overt, partly internal, with others."[6] The self-determination of the different individual and group identities sharing a territory and their interaction can only happen within the context of this kind of dialogical relation. Once democracy has replaced imposed violence, dialogue becomes the key element in multiculturalism. But how are we to understand this dialogue? For the word can create an illusion. Whatever the concrete schema proposed, it refers to an exchange involving two terms, to simplify let's say culture A and culture B. Multiculturalism would thus be a situation where cultures originating elsewhere encounter the indigenous culture or cultures in democratic interchange. The encounter itself isn't new, since as we have seen peoples have always intermixed, but in our democratic societies, this encounter is attempted under the aegis of dialogue rather than violence. Innovation lies herein: a dialogue of words and recognition replace force and contempt.

Now, this popular way of looking at things actually ignores the key element of dialogue, and thus condemns a fair number of encounters to sterility or even to taking two steps backward into confrontation and violence. Daily life is full of examples of how violence endures. It takes more than just bringing people together, even if it's in a modern and democratic country, to make violence disappear and dialogue emerge.[7]

In reality, as long as the proposed values are viewed as the other culture, or the culture of the other, they risk being rejected. This is an example of a binary pattern. Dialogue with the other can only be seen in terms of domination or surrender: impose my identity on him or give up mine. But what happens in *mestizaje* is a whole new ball game: it's a physical dialogue involving three, not two, terms: one, the other, and what unites them and is born of their encounter. This is the most concrete of all reminders that all dialogue, if it is to be an interhuman dialogue, requires a third party or element to which the two protagonists refer. Otherwise, it's just about confrontation.

Considering the encounter between cultures to be a kind of dialogue supposes that we accord this dialogue the dimension and conditions required for it to be truly interhuman. Not a dialogue reduced to exchanging the usual, well-meaning empty words and phrases (often just what is meant by dialogue) which only leads to a dissolution of all thought and all identity, but an exchange between two terms implying a third one, the "excluded" third party, who is not a participant in the dialogue but who makes it possible and constitutes its objective. The *he, she,* or *it* that the *I* and the *you* talk about:

> During dialogue, he or she, it or they indicate a third element, excluded from or external to the closed space of our dialogue, a non-membership in our communication, a surplus, him, her, it, them, without whom, without which or again about whom or about which we are talking, a third element excluded and included.[8]

Michel Serres, a standard bearer for *mestizaje,* adds: "This is equally true for raising the body and for educating. The Mestizo here is called the educated-third." Michel Serres focuses on upbringing and instruction, the apprenticeship of a *he/it* surpassing the *I* and the *you* of teacher and student, commanding their dialogue and over which, in the end, they have no control. The "excluded third"—a concept in logic and not meaning social exclusion—is what makes dialogue possible between partners. Without a third term, the "third," present, no dialogue between two people is possible. What Michel Serres says about education is valid for all dialogue and for dialogue between cultures. The latter often takes the form of a long road traveled together, a pedagogy. This dialogue between cultures cannot be envisioned between only two terms; it would quickly become a sterile or violent face-to-face standoff. As with all dialogue, the dialogue between cultures requires a third term, a "third" making it possible and productive.

The mestizo is this "third"—individual, cultural element, or situation—the mestizo third party, making communication possible, the factor over which the dialogue's two protagonists ultimately have no sway. Dialogue, in effect, is possible and fertile only once a "new being" born of their encounter is present and accepted by both protagonists. A new language, a new experience, a new relation: something new is being fashioned in common, a situation or an invention that the exchange will produce. Something in which both protagonists will recognize themselves and, at the same time, something totally new compared to each of them. Thus "mestizo" in intercultural dialogue would be the third, excluded yet present, thanks to which interchange and the transformation of the protagonists is possible.

Mestizo would be what is born of this exchange: child, new mix, new culture. The only solution for getting past violence.

Archaic societies managed violence by kidnapping and exchanging women.[9] Our societies offer dialogue as an alternative to war. But dialogue, if it's a two-party standoff, only keeps violence alive. It becomes a tit-for-tat, two-term equation, condemned to an inflation of words and leaving no room for innovation or for the transformation of the protagonists, except maybe by entrenching them in their positions. It leads to compromises that are necessarily only temporary. It doesn't indicate toward what kind of future energy can be directed. In short, it's entrapment in a mortal duo, whereas life is ternary, or even better, to use Dany-Robert Dufour's expression, trinity.[10] This author makes the choice between binary or ternary crucial for the survival of our societies. From this perspective, the mestizo would represent, in the dialogue between cultures in any given territory, what makes encounter possible. For the multicultural societies that ours are becoming, the mestizo would represent the excluded third pointing to the future. The mestizo, whether individual or group, is the fruit promised and engendered by multicultural societies. But the thing is, this mestizo fruit doesn't belong to any of the different original cultures. He or she is often named for one or the other, classified in one or the other, and thereby betrayed. As Virgil Elizondo writes:

> The Mestizo cannot adequately be defined by the categories of his/her groups of origin. His/her identity doesn't belong to one story only, doesn't fit into one set of norms only. . . . We are the in-between people, for our existence includes elements of our dual origin without our being completely one or the other. This in-between identity also give us prodigious creative potential.(11)

The In-between Zones

And so the possibility of new zones appears, mestizo zones, "third," as it were, wedging themselves in between easily recognized reference points or cultural markers, upsetting bonds, memberships. They are new loci where creativity can grow; new because it's impossible to reduce them to former ties and memberships: mestizo forms are not a reproduction of their origins. New also because turned toward the future and because it's impossible to predict what aspect they'll take. The emergence or appearance of something mestizo is always a "newness." The arts as we've seen are one of the privileged areas of this emergence. Music, fashion, the plastic arts meld each day undreamed-of forms, colors, melodies for our enchantment. Cuisine, and in general, the multiple bonds of friendship and family, as well as social ties that weave the fabric of life in society are also mingled. Life in society becomes mestizo slowly but surely. Multiculturalism is vibrant and transforms society's forms.

Is it possible to foresee the forms this transformation will take? The often-heard question: "Where will it all stop?," implicitly conforms the phenomenon but also dissimulates old fears. There suddenly emerge new ways of life, new group tendencies, new value choices heretofore unknown. It's the case for instance with certain family or religious customs. Should they be, in the name of interculturalism and its accompanying *mestizaje*, accepted and legitimated, or, on the contrary, refused in the name of traditional, familiar forms? We know that Taylor asked this question at the end of his essay and put forward the notion of a middle road between the conformity of all individuals to one unique model and the self-immurement of each group within its own way of seeing and doing things.[12] Are there any criteria that would help us imagine this "middle road," which in fact will be a new road?

The primary characteristic of the forms produced by the encounter between cultures is that they are novel. But this novelty or newness is often perceived, at least to begin with, as having a negative charge—as are mestizo individuals who are neither one nor the other of their parents; who neither completely recognize themselves nor are fully recognized on either side of the border. Consequently, the reflex reaction is rejection, with the accompanying risk that everyone shuts themselves in their own world and opposes custom to custom, life choice to life choice, value to value. This way we find ourselves once more in a binary situation, meaning face-to-face standoff and confrontation. Democracy invites something quite different. Under its auspices, the situation becomes ternary, a triangle formed by the different cultures sharing a territory and the "something new" generated by their encounter. This kind of dialogue enables exorcizing fears and translates democracy's values into reality, bringing democracy closer. *Mestizaje*, the outgrowth of dialogue, engenders concrete "possibles." It proposes a dynamics of transformation.

If we refer to the models mentioned earlier, especially the model whose underpinning is common citizenship and where cultural specificities are relegated to the realm of individual choice, implementing a ternary dialogue doesn't seem very difficult. The mestizo has a right to exist, in the same way any citizen does. The fact that exclusions or violence continue to exist is simply the symptom of an imperfect democracy, the residue of former inequalities, the result of a wanting civic sense or education. Successful integration is meant to smooth out these kinds of knots and jags. For democracy is neutral with respect to different cultural traditions. It establishes a bond of a specific nature that doesn't of itself compete with the traditional bonds of family, religion, and ethnic group embodied in any given culture. The choices made regarding these traditional bonds are of no concern to democracy unless they interfere with its laws, which precisely represent the considerable, daily stakes involved in learning citizenship. In this view, it is not the law's role to recognize the mestizo in any specific manner, just as it is not its role to specifically recognize any other particular group.

Nevertheless it remains true that, precisely in everyday situations, a paradox suddenly appears. In one way, democracy is a kind of abstract principle. In another way, democracy is in fact embodied in concrete forms in any given territory. These social and political forms embodying democracy are influenced by history, tradition, and by elements of cultural heritage, itself a consequence of multiple instances of *mestizaje*. In summary, it is only if democracy is implemented that it can be apprehended. It is a principle at work in concrete legal, political, and social forms. It can't be isolated like a chemical substance. It assumes the specific aspect of this particular nation and this particular law. The nation represents on any given territory, a certain number of specific choices at any given time. The law is their translation. The ensuing risk, depending upon which branch of the paradox we chose—abstract principle or concrete forms—is that either the law doesn't interfere with the particular cultures or that its concrete applications do interfere with them. Consequently, conflicts arise opposing law to law, custom to custom, and in short, reintroducing vestiges of the former empires into the very heart of democratic societies. And reducing the debate to a binary one.

The only solution at this point is to make place for a third term, beyond the two terms present in the debate: this term is the "something new" to be crafted. Now, democratic law states it simply: there is one common and universal law and it is the same for all individuals. Its universal ambition is precisely what makes democratic law different from all other laws. Democratic law wants to be, here and now, the concrete translation of human rights. It's in the name of human rights that the foreigner is given a place and accorded the same rights as any other human being. Human rights, translated in law, are what make mutual recognition and the commingling of different human groups (*mestizaje*) possible.

This encounter presupposes that each group adheres to the common democratic law. The law's formulation remains the same, whether the issue is debate over the daily relations between neighbors or what status to grant the large ethnic or religious groups, for instance. The law thus represents, for the cultures present in any given territory, the tool that not only makes *mestizaje* possible but guarantees what all cultures aspire to: identity, universality, and defusing violence. Each human group is specific, yet at the same time each human group considers itself a universal model. For its members, the group represents humanity brought close and personal and it also nourishes feelings of dignity, of belonging to a universal humanity. This dual aspect—personal and universal—is indispensable for the survival of both groups and individuals. This common horizon of universality, translated by human rights and the concrete applications of democratic law, makes encounter and recognition possible. Now, the apprenticeship by individuals and society of this aspiration to universality needs constant renewal. Because for a human being to fully exist, his or her particularisms must receive recognition, and society is full of colors, variety, differences. This is what constitutes its wealth. The opposite, a society of identical individuals, clones, would not just be unlivable, it would be sinister. The task of articulating particularisms with democratic law's horizon of universality is thus essential.

The new loci mentioned earlier are where this articulation of particularisms and universality happens. First and foremost, these "spaces" have an educational function: in them it's possible to talk about our differences, place them in perspective, and move beyond them. These spaces enable breaking out of Manichean duality squaring off in two columns all that opposes *us* and *them*, conveniently forgetting that *us* also designates a specific culture nevertheless required to aim at the horizon of universality. Creative spaces: here particularisms can be manifested without fear, yet at the same time are called upon to conform to democracy's universal aim. These loci are places of transformation where both individuals and groups can risk themselves at the new experiences and the freedom that, when all is said and done, they desire, signifying by their presence here their acceptance of modern societies' social contract. Numerous teachers and other concerned individuals (social workers, volunteers, religious authorities, etc.) act daily as intermediaries. And many groups, clubs, and associations fashion a civil society where their members can create their future. These spaces become an interface where interchange between groups is possible and where each individual is oriented toward the common goal.

This common goal is now no longer abstract, nor is it imposed, becoming an expression of one culture's domination over the other, "minority" cultures, attitudes which just serve to freeze the process and in the end betray it and reveal themselves inadequate. The common goal becomes a subject of daily debate under democracy's wing, enabling recognition, without discrimination of any kind, of each person's status as a citizen, that is to say, as a universal subject, and at the same time as an individual with all the richness of his or her specific personality. From one citizen to the other, from one group to the other bonds are forged, shifting bonds, mestizo bonds, creative bonds, generating innovation in society. In this way, a kind of *mestizaje* can be crafted that is not inegalitarian.

Should we go further and evoke *mestizaje* on a wider scale, on a planetary scale? This hypothesis is rejected by some thinkers, like Samuel P. Huntington.[13] In his book, *The Clash of Civilizations and the Remaking of World Order*, he presents a table grouping peoples and showing the relations, alliances, or confrontations taking shape between them, relations in which the questions of cultural identity occupy a preponderant place. According to Huntington, the importance of political borders is diminishing compared to ethnic and cultural borders. "Civilizational wars" threaten to replace political wars.

The information and examples Huntington furnishes about the way culture and cultural identity are gaining importance are impressive. An illustration of this in daily life is that there hardly exists an intercultural encounter where the subject of identity is not broached. The subject of identity cannot be separated from other major currents affecting our world, currents that are omnipresent today because information spans all borders. Humanity is in the midst of "universalization," and no group can resist this movement. Formerly, ancient texts considered that the world's ordering was the handiwork of the gods. Modern ideologies, not just Marxism but close to us the liberal ideology of globalization, have shifted the center but still claim to organize the world. For it is necessary to have a core center. In fact, many core centers exist: those of the past still around and even enjoying renewed vigour; those of the present, causing conflicts between universalisms: religious or revolutionary, economic or political. Each one of these centers makes a claim to universality. Each center can survive only by affirming its specificities and excluding the other. So, in this case, the desire for human universality can only survive through affirming itself in particularisms, leading automatically to reactions of exclusion. We encounter once again, but on a worldwide scale, the same paradox of the universal and the particular we saw earlier concerning individuals. And the people who live next to us, the ones we cross on street corners every day, are inhabited by internal worlds that exclude one another, an omen of wars in the making. Huntington is not optimistic. Unable to resist being systematic, he considers cultures as unmoving blocks in opposition to each other. He is extremely concerned that the worst can happen.

Nevertheless, these people live in the same territory, and share the elements of a common vocabulary. For example, in the French Republic's bicentennial of 1989, I participated in a university seminar group studying how "human rights" were given expression in the major cultural areas of our planet, for they all make reference to human rights. Texts about human rights exist in religions—even the fundamentalists mention them—in Marxism, as well as in the countries of Europe and North and South America. No one today wants to be left out when it comes to applying or respecting human rights. Yet at the same time, everyone is eager to prove that this universal ambition can only be fully realized within their own specific cultural tradition: Christian, Moslem, Liberal, or Marxist. Being conscious of this attitude can lead to skepticism or lassitude, as can the debates at U.N. forums that never seem to produce any results. But it also indicates an essential point: even if accompanied by ambiguity, everyone accepts at least the principle of a common expression, *human rights,* explicitly stated in the United Nation's declaration of 1948. All accept too the principle of a common aspiration—at least no one dares openly to deny it. And so exchange, dialogue, become possible, in the absence of which we'd have outright war.

Huntington does consider that what he calls "*an end to civilizational wars*" is possible. He sees mediation as its instrument, not mediation of neutral organizations but of middle-level "*interested parties*" who have gained the support of their immediate group and have the ability to negotiate agreements with their opposite number on the one hand and on the other, convince their group to accept these agreements.[14] Here, unexpectedly reintroduced into international diplomacy, appear elements pertaining to bonds with one's immediate group, mestizo bonds. There's truth in the old saying: mestizos have always made great double agents. But here it's the opposite; the role is of mediator, not double agent. Groups or individuals, the mestizo is an interface, creating contact between intimate enemies. This is the price of peace. In other words, the alternative to war is in these "mestizo" bonds woven along the edges of cultures and enabling a different "space" to begin to exist.

Then, is the choice between "*mestizaje* or barbary" to quote another book title?[15] Either we consider cultures as hermetically sealed entities, and the results are wars but also, in the long term, the demise of culture itself, or cultures accept mutual recognition and encounter with others, with the risk of transformation and hence of a certain form of death; but this engenders something new. Accepting *mestizaje* for a culture means risking death and ensuring its survival.

Here is what *mestizaje* is about: it pushes to their extreme limits the paradoxes of social bonds. It bares what is at stake at different levels in the encounter with the other, the stranger/foreigner, and ultimately in every encounter as well. *Mestizaje*, always unpredictable, slips itself into the precise order and harmony of established social bonds. It loosens up too-rigid identities. This makes *mestizaje* a fertile element in society, an element which, even disclaimed, makes society progress. Through its sole existence, *mestizaje* opens up a new zone. It offers the opportunity for new openings and invites us to pay the price. It's not surprising that *mestizaje* provokes fear and attraction, the two faces of desire. A more vast zone, more murky and more elusive it's true, superimposes itself on the narrow borderlines of maps—a zone shaped by the connections humans weave with each other. It is a zone equally shaped by the phantasms, dreams, and symbols present in people's conscious and unconscious imaginations.

Notes

1. Hillary RODHAM CLINTON, *Civiliser la démocratie*, Paris, Desclée de Brouwer, 1998.

2. Cf. the remarkable work by Xavier DE PLANHOL, *Géographie historique de la France,* Paris, Fayard, 1988.

3. On cultural transformations in North America, see Joël GARREAU, *The nine Nations of North America*, New York, Avon, 1981.

4. On cultural identities in France, cf. Emmanuel TODD, *L'invention de la France*, Paris, Livre de Poche, Pluriel num. 8365, 1981.

5. On the modern concept of nation, cf. Dominique SCHNAPPER, *La communauté des citoyens*, Paris, Gallimard, 1994.

6. Cf. Charles TAYLOR, op. cit., pg. 34.

7. Here is what a high school principal has to say: "The word 'integration' is considered a magical mantra: chant it enough and order as well as the pax republicana will reign. And even then, it would be useful if this word had at least a minimum of meaning. When people talk integration to us, what is it they are talking about?" Jacques CROISIER, professor of philosophy at the Dammarie-les-Lys high school, "Les rebelles de la mondialisation," in *Le Monde,* January 16, 1998.

8. Michel SERRES, *Le tiers-Instruit,* Paris, François Bourin, 1991, pg. 82:

> Au cours du dialogue, il ou elle, cela, elles ou ils désignent, en tiers justement, l'excusion ou l'extérieur de l'ensemble clos de notre entretien, la non-appartenance à notre communication, tierce place donc, plus, en precision, celui, celle, cela, celles ou ceux, sans qui, sans quoi, ou de qui et de quoi nous parlons, tiers exclu et inclus.

9. Cf. Pierre CLASTRES, *Archéologie de la violence, la guerre dans les sociétés primitives*, Paris, l'Aube, 1997.

10. Dany-Robert DUFOUR, *Les mystères de la Trinité*, Paris, Gallimard, 1990.

11. Virgil ELIZONDO, op. cit., pg. 156.

12. Cf. Charles TAYLOR, op. cit., pg. 72.

13. Samuel P. HUNTINGTON, *Le Choc des Civilisations*, Paris, Odile Jacob, 1997.

14. Ibid., pg. 325.

15. René DUBOUX, *Métissage ou barbarie*, Paris, L'Harmattan, 1994.

~

CHAPTER EIGHT

Symbology Shattered

As societal relations continue their ceaseless Brownian movement, in each individual resonates a barely acknowledged cortege of emotions, astonishments, or anxieties spurred by the encounter with the other. Individuals have an internal world that is the other side of the face they turn to society. It is not an inexpressible universe—for it does express itself through words and gestures—it is a personal universe. In one respect it's almost incommunicable since it affects our identity, that bubbling and inexhaustible spring from which it becomes possible to say "*I*." In another aspect, though, the language and the symbols expressing this universe are the same for the other members of our group, our family, or the people from "our neck of the woods." The *I* and the *we*, the permanent interchange between people, are organized by them and they in turn order the world through the major collective symbols that structure personal and group identity. We carry these symbols within, where they operate without our even being aware; they have been imprinted in our being since the beginning of our lives, not just through words but through the gestures and attitudes that surrounded us and accompanied our growth. The world of symbols forms for individuals the world they inhabit, the solid ground upon which they stand, the anchor for their security and dreams, the place of their anxiety or gratification.

The encounter with the stranger/foreigner suddenly shakes this feeling of solidity and security. It feels as if the ground were falling away. Our cultural reference points don't seem as clear-cut anymore. The world is no longer unity, it loses its consistency, because other humans, elsewhere and with different choices, have undertaken things in a different way and inhabit other symbolic worlds. Where to place them, where to place ourselves? The discovery of America was probably the greatest shock of symbols history has ever experienced and also the most tragic.[1] But this encounter holds something exemplary since it would forge modern *mestizaje*. On both sides it was a shock, and the encounter's violence, as well as the astonishment due to its unprecedented nature, have been described many times. The reactions to this encounter cover the entire range of attitudes, from the conquistador's swaggering assurance, convinced of his legitimacy and unheedingly trampling the symbolic world of the other, to the receptivity of an anti-conquistador like Cabeza de Vaca. When writing to the king of Spain, after wandering eight years among tribes on the Gulf coast, Cabeza de Vaca tells him: "All these peoples must be treated well, it is the most unerring way, and there is no other."[2] And, as one of his commentators quotes him, "Everything we learned on the other side of the seas [in Spain], we rejected. The only thing that remained with us, for our salvation and the salvation of others, is what we learned in our Mother's arms."[3]

In our multicultural societies, daily encounter is no doubt less spectacular. But it touches the same zones and requires the same receptivity, unless violence is to reappear. How to explain, for instance, racism's recurrent reappearance in our democratic societies, despite law, education, and widespread information, unless it is the case that ultimately, racism activates ancient fears, triggers anew irrational fantasies, and awakens phantoms that we thought eradicated by the influence of rationality. An individual who claims to be nonracist, and who truly wants to be, suddenly notices behavior and attitudes reappearing in him he thought had disappeared. This is proof that underlying areas remain as yet unlit, precisely those areas of deeply entrenched symbols that are perturbed by the transformations in our societies. Each encounter really takes place on several levels. Although occurring within a framework of rules and regulations, it's not limited to these. Each encounter also mobilizes all the images, values, attitudes we use to express our identity. It perturbs and antagonizes them and, in the end, calls into question our symbolic world.

Nebulous Images

The first effect of the encounter between cultures is to make one's own identity and the other's identity less distinct. Some time ago, in one of Montreal's outlying neighborhoods, I witnessed an unusual sight: a line of colorfully decorated floats accompanied by a highly colorful crowd. I was informed that the Indian community, a very sizable one in Montreal, was celebrating one of its tutelary gods. These were no doubt the same men and women whom fellow citizens mixed with at work, at school, or in their shops. They were neighbors, citizens, yet this festival suddenly revealed them as partly different, coming from another, less comprehensible world. As the decorated images, surrounded by flower-strewing children and followed by a singing, laughing crowd, meandered through the streets, surprised or blasé passersby watched what was obviously for them a curious event. A mix of bewilderment and curiosity could be read on their faces, but also a certain fascination, like when one attends a forbidden spectacle. Some people moved away while continuing to watch. Others ostensibly turned their backs, yet others pretended indifference. What did they perceive? An ancient exoticism, a menace for public order? Maybe, but also a festival atmosphere whose equivalent is becoming rare. And all the while, the procession continued going by, tranquil and secure in their legitimate right to be doing just what they were doing.

The most conspicuous facets of multiculturalism were on show here, ones that have theoretically hardly any importance or existence, except in people's private lives, but also those facets we cannot fail to notice, whether it's a Moslem marriage, Chinese New Year, or the Portuguese community's procession in a small French town in honor of Our Lady of Fatima. These are facets that everyone else considers the neighbor's affair. "They" celebrate Ramadan or Yom Kippur. We remark on the associated bizarreness, solemnity, or gaiety, but *"It's their affair, not ours."* Parallel to public and professional life, multiple currents circulate, linked to family, associations, religion, that are the other face of collective existence. These currents feed identity, and enable us to say *I* or *we* by claiming membership in a specific group or tradition. For individuals, they constitute the most secure area and the one most necessary to their existence. Evoking the multicultural nature of our societies is not simply a matter of acknowledging the great variety of groups coexisting on the same territory. More importantly, it is a matter of recognizing that each of these groups claims a right to specific life-choices, possesses and claims as their own specific outlooks on life, behavior and feelings, all of which make up their identity. Social diversity echoes personal differences coming from as many mutually independent, mutually exclusive, even opposing, symbolic worlds.

These elements are being challenged, threatened, and sorely tested by multicultural encounters. Difference easily becomes disqualification, or at the very least, nonrecognition. This is apparent with religious calendars. Each group follows its specific calendar. There are Jewish holidays and Christian and Moslem ones, and slowly but surely other calendars are added, all within the common Republican calendar. But the precise point is that none of these particular calendars can claim to apply to everyone, and as a result, the former harmony that in our European countries existed between the rhythm of symbolic (i.e. religious) time and secular time is daily further dissolved. Now, this harmony was an identity factor. Today's dissociation of the different calendars fills some with nostalgia, or with sadness, or sometimes with fear, fear of the threat of losing one's marks, one's identity. Hence the discourse on identity, about recovering former unity, restoring lost harmony, recreating a world of unified resemblance, even at the cost of immurement. Such attempts are in vain because the world we live in is henceforward pluralistic.

Each point in our world of symbols can thus become a place of uncertainty. The images are scrambled. What seemed solid becomes fragile: time, space, relationships. The symbolic world vacillates. Identity gets fractured. "*I'm not from here and I'm not from there.*" This oft-heard phrase underlines the split in identity of the person who has a foot in the door of several worlds. It also underlines the secret wound often present. We're not talking here about culture viewed externally as an ensemble of curiosities characterizing the other, the one who's different, but about culture as experienced internally as what gives me my own identity and without which it would be impossible for me to say "*I am.*" But the "*I am*" loses its unity here. Or to put it another way, "*I have become a stranger to myself.*" The tension of conflicting cultures is inscribed within each individual.

This is a painful, sometimes violent tension for the newly arrived immigrant who experiences it for the first time. He or she doesn't find it possible to renounce certain traits rightly considered as having helped to forge self-identity up until now. But the tension is also felt by the person already present, the non-newcomer, who more or less feels threatened by the person to whom he or she opens the door. Both of the protagonists are affected. In fact, no one escapes this tension, except by shutting themselves up in the bastion of their certitudes. Everyone, in one way or another, is an actor in cultural conflict. Because one fine day established borders are subverted. For example, borders are transgressed when there's a marriage between members of two different groups, or simply at school where children discover the diversity of the world they live in. Just listen: remarks, warnings, fears, fascination, follow closely upon each other. Each person sees the image of his own identity questioned and threatened simultaneously. A dormant area in normal circumstances, but never asleep, it wakens, watchful, at the slightest sign of difference.

The mestizo is the most vigorously exacerbated focus for these tensions, carrying them internally like a personal fracture. The mestizo's "non-identity," to use Elizondo's word, is simply how the violence in the relations between his/her two ancestral cultures translates. But this non-identity creates a resonance with the surrounding environment. The fracture continues operating in the major areas of existence, precisely those areas where the threat will be the most acutely felt, where resistance will take hold. There are three specific areas: marriage and family, religion and ritual, cuisine and domestic life. Areas of resistance but also of *mestizaje*. They are present in every survey. The symbolic world crystallizes around them. They are the locus of the early attitudes and gestures that model children from their birth in order to produce vital adults, integrated into their group. It's in these areas too that growing children discover and affirm their differences and assert autonomy. The body is connected to all three areas.

The Body at Stake

The indistinctness of self-images echoes the image of the body, the way people—since everyone is affected—perceive the body. The body is the ultimate stake "at stake." The body is where in the last resort symbols take root, where the encounter of identities as well as the possible forms of *mestizaje* of cultures are acted out. The body is also where immurement originates, where ideals topple, where violence suddenly appears. The body's ambiguity, endured or dissipated, governs encounters, today more than ever.

Encountering the other means crossing a border, always a physical experience. The body is an actor here through food and language, through the entire set of gestures and behaviors. However willing we are, we'll never be as fluent in the foreigner's language as we are in our mother tongue. There will always be a little something—accent or phrasing—to disclose our difference. And the charms of exotic dishes sometimes produce unexpected effects. These introductory experiences are there to remind us that communicating is a way of being open to new discoveries and new landscapes, but at the same time, they bring us up against our own physical limits. The body mirrors for individuals their own specificity. One discovers that one is circumscribed within the boundaries of one's own body. It's impossible to do everything or to speak all languages or to try all the possibilities offered. The body energetically reminds us that there is no humanity without difference, first and foremost geographical and physical differences. The enthusiasm about interculturalism is tempered by material possibilities and comes up against the ambivalence characterizing every human endeavor involving the bodily dimensions of time and space.

This is because the borders of an individual's body, like any border, simultaneously close off and open up. The body is where the sense of connectedness to society is forged, in all its specificity and concrete reality. An individual's body is where, simultaneously, the other is encountered and one's distinct identity discovered, where there is an opening up to exchange with others and a sealing off into insurmountable solitude. Crossing a geographical or social border helps to get a grasp on one's personal identity. We discover ourselves when we are "abroad," and it's through the stranger/foreigner that we increase self-knowledge.

And so, symbolic exchange occurs between our body and our social bonds that determine our way of "being present in/to the world." It is therefore impossible to oppose, the way classical thought did, the individual's specific body—permeable monad, sealed off and isolated from others—to the group and to society. The two are simultaneously in play, and the vocabulary of relationships to others borrows images, symbols, attitudes, or taboos from the body. The body's boundary and society's boundary thus create a resonance. The same codes and words go back and forth from one area to the other, awakening the same wonder or expressing the same fears.

This process of resonance is taken to the extreme in the encounter with a stranger/foreigner, the social, political, and cultural boundaries creating a resonance with the body's boundary, underlining differences in red ink. But why are they so often experienced as menacing? How to explain why this process is so often negatively connoted? Why does the encounter with the other fan fear and rejection? And how to explain that, after decades of education about democratic values, discourses on exclusion based on a physical rejection of the other, a rejection of the other's bodily presence, are once again flourishing?

The vocabulary of exclusion from society often alludes to the body. Alongside expressions linked to geographical space, "chez nous," "chez eux" ("our home," "our place"; "their home," their place"), a series of other expressions exists that only make sense in relation to the body, and especially to the notion of the body's purity. We've already touched upon vocabulary referring to the *blood's purity*, like *mixed blood*, or to the idea of *racial purity* or to the *purity of language*. We need to add to them, expressions that have sadly become all-too-frequently heard, like the expressions referring to *ethnic purification*. All these expressions have a history. Some have left shameful, painful traces. Their consequences are still with us and their devastating effects continue. We don't have to look very far before finding one or the other becoming ideology, fully accepted and shaping policy. The *purity of blood* represented an ideal for some in sixteenth-century Spain, just after the Reconquista. *Racial purity* was one of the key elements in Nazi ideology, and *ethnic purification* continues to have fans in Europe and on other continents, and we all know at what cost. All these atrocious situations reveal the bottomless pits waiting on the edges of a world of symbols perverted.

Expressions and attitudes of ordinary life can seem far removed from such a world. Nevertheless they share the same symbolic roots. These pejorative expressions echo a vision of humanity divided into two groups by a subtle and invisible line: the pure and the impure. This kind of pattern has infinite declensions, for there exist various signs of purity, and first of all, cleanliness. As a result, foreigners are said to be *dirty, badly dressed,* they are *ill-mannered* and *speak incorrectly.* And from body to moral character, it's a thin line: they are *lazy,* have *bad behavior,* are *disorderly* and finally, *depraved* and *dangerous.* Consequently the foreigner's presence presents a risk of *contamination.* His or her morals, decried as dissolute, are *contagious,* and self-protection is necessary. All these expressions, overheard in daily life or read in a certain kind of literature, reflect stereotypes involving first and foremost the body, stereotypes thus transposed from an individual body to the language of the social body, that is, of social relations. Consequently, it's not simply a matter of plays on words or superficial stereotypes we can laugh at and shrug off. We're dealing in this daily language with the quality of the relationship to others, with respect shown for the other's identity as well as for one's own. These kinds of thought patterns activate codes of *purity* and *defilement, health* and *depravity,* and ultimately, *matter* and *spirit.*

Purity, as the "Quest for an Absolute Endangering our Humanity," to quote the title of the review "*Autrement,*"[4] means the ambition of an identity excluding any admixture. Early on for the small child, this ambition is imprinted in the body in the form of a demand for cleanliness. Acquiring purity/cleanliness will require a long apprenticeship from the little human being. For children, this apprenticeship is the condition for gaining control over their own body, for learning that they are separate from objects, from others, and to begin with, from the maternal body. To exist is thus to be separate, to be capable of recognizing a border between one's own body and the other's body, to emerge from fusion anxiety, both fascinating and threatening. In this sense, to exist means being oneself without admixture, being complete, being pure. Purity becomes the equivalent of control over self, identified with perfection.

It's not surprising then that religions will elevate purity to an ideal. Ritual purity separates the world of gods from the world of humans and draws the boundary between the sacred and the profane. Social purity in some traditions serves as the basis for establishing a hierarchy and organizing society. Spiritual purity represents personal renewal, both psychological renewal and renewal of identity. Education, at least in the West, is predicated in our modern age on the meaning of purity. This purity, often referring uniquely to sexual purity, becomes respect for the body, one's own and the other's. For Christianity, purity is the *sine qua non* condition for a love relationship to be valid, as well as charity; simply put, it's a prerequisite for salvation. A doctrine on purity, both precise and radical, was developed over centuries in the old catechisms. Radical, because this doctrine left no alternative. In matters of purity, there are no halfway measures, and sins of impurity are automatically considered very serious indeed. Precise, because this doctrine explicitly indicated how things should be done, meaning not done. The texts went on in great detail about the occasions leading to impurity, including thought itself. The code of *pure* and *impure* applies to every aspect of existence. Purity is closely associated with identity, and specifically with a notion of identity implying interior self-possession.

Ordinary language in the West continues to associate purity with whiteness. As François Madeiros has shown, colonization/civilization, supported by the preachings and teachings of its religious orders, rooted the phantasm of a purity/white connection in the minds of people.

> Africa: Aethiops, this was the name given to the inhabitants of this far away land. This Greek word meaning "burned face" clearly shows the connection made between the color black applied to a person's skin and this immense land permanently spewing fire and never burning itself out. The influence of Christianity on thinking in the Middle Ages easily enables us to imagine the symbolic function of Aethiops, keeping in mind the dichotomy of human destiny on Earth—pure and impure— and in the heavens—Paradise and hell. In the collective imagination, Aethiops thus appears to be the materialization of the "black sins" leading straight to hell whose inhabitants are burned.[5]

These kinds of thought patterns take a long time to change. So, we have a chain whose links are: purity, light, spirit, white opposed to another chain: black, matter, obscurity, impurity. Two things that bear equal witness to how deeply entrenched and abiding these associations are, are the nineteenth-century preaching that considered both Indians and blacks demons, and the contemporary discourse on purity of blood resurfacing in Europe. It's a thin line between impurity and degeneration, and Gobineau crossed it, as we've seen. For him, human societies are characterized by the process of degeneration they are undergoing. According to him, "degenerate" peoples exist due to the *mestizaje* they have undergone, and consequently, they are of lesser value than "healthy" peoples and must rightfully be dominated by them.

The *body/spirit* dichotomy further reinforces the separations between pure and impure, healthy and degenerate. Even if, according to Vigarello,[6] we've outgrown this Platonic pattern, it still is engrained in vocabulary. Things connected with the body are spontaneously classified in the column "matter," opposed to what is connected to "spirit" or "intellect." Since the other, impure and degenerate, is considered someone uncivilized, coarse, human encounters can only happen on an intellectual, that is, pure and spiritual, level and are naturally accompanied by a condescending attitude. The very expression *intercultural* often implies that encountering the other takes place on a cultural level—intellectual and rather aseptic—in this way ignoring the less ethereal aspects of the encounters between humans.

> There's no question that the old Platonic tradition of the body "prison of the soul" has lost all legitimacy. The body was doubly rejected in this tradition: it foiled any true knowledge, opposing a prison of the senses; it perverted all attempts at morality through the attraction to pleasure. Authentic thought was first of all a refusal, a deliberate opposition to the body, a conquest imposed "through thought alone, through thought without any admixture," in order to better undertake the "search for each reality." (Phedon). This view made conscience a sovereign instance and the body a dreaded resistance: an obstacle on the road to Truth, an obstacle on the road to Good. The Christian tradition will adopt and adapt this separation, the body becoming less an organism and more a "flesh," the flesh that any effort at liberation must transcend.[7]

Our societies having become less religious and more secular hasn't done away with the desires and fears connected with purity. Perhaps today these fears take other shapes. Hygiene and fear of physical contact, odors, and germs can easily substitute for the obsessions about purity in ancient texts. But above all, fear of the stranger/foreigner remains tied to infantile attitudes, indivisible desire of personification and dissolution. As Julia Kristeva writes:

> In truth it is rare that a foreigner arouses the same terrifying anguish as death, the female vagina or the "maleficent" unbridled passion. Are we so sure however that the "political" feelings of xenophobia do not contain, often unconsciously, this trance of terrified jubilation said to be unheimlich, that the English call uncanny, and the Greeks simply . . . xenos, "stranger." In the fascinated rejection that the foreigner provokes in us, there is a disturbing component of strangeness in the sense of the depersonalization that Freud discovered and which connects with our infantile desires and fears of the other, the other of death, the other of femaleness, the other of uncontrollable pulsions. The stranger is within us, we are battling against our proper unconscious—this "improper" of our impossible "proper."[8]

In our opinion, it is these infantile attitudes rooted in the deep zones of psyche that explain why stereotypes about foreigners are so radical and violent. The primary sources of energy feeding racism can be found in infantile fears concerning the body's integrity and cohesion. The other, simply by being other, different, is seen as terrifying. He/She frightens and threatens to destroy us. With this viewpoint, even the slightest difference provokes violence, be it skin color or sexual difference. There naturally flows from this a domination/desire relation, built on violence and illustrated by the revolting practice of collective rape that recent conflicts on different continents have caused to re-emerge. We find ourselves in the presence of revived archaic attitudes. As Paul Ricoeur remarks,

> The fear of the impure . . . relates to the diminution of existence, the loss of a personal core. . . . The representation of defilement remains in the light and shadow of a quasi-physical infection pointing toward a quasi-moral indignity. This ambiguity is not expressed conceptually, but experienced intentionally through the very quality of the fear, half-physical, half-ethical, adhering to the representation of the impure.[9]

According to him, we're dealing with a primitive fear, existing before the separation of the ethic and the physical and possessing as it were a "pre-ethical" nature. It's the role and task of the verb to go beyond this fear and sublimate it.

By transposing to the realm of social bonds what is a bodily attribute, words like *health, illness, degeneracy* become categories purporting to judge society and the relation to others. They reintroduce a binary logic we've already met. People are healthy or ill, the way they are colored or white, pure or impure, in short, the right kind of person or dangerous. Through these types of categories, a subject's individual identity and integrity are directly linked to his/her refusal of relations with others, with the other, with the stranger/foreigner. It's no longer possible for language to play a mediating role. A rudimentary ideology takes the place of dialogue. Recognition trips over manicheism.

History has seen human groups having built their identity on a world vision and attitudes connected to the notion of purity. Originally the noun *Puritans* meant a rigorist religious group following Calvin's teachings that appeared in England at the end of the sixteenth century. Some of its members emigrated to America at the beginning of the seventeenth century. But the adjective *puritan* continues to designate a certain kind of attitude regarding others and the world, a claim to a certain moral or doctrinal rigor, a desire for integrity, for purity. Now in Weber's analysis of historical Puritanism, this attitude is translated by a certain form of rationality applied to all societal relations. Max Weber has shown its coherence and uncovered how such an attitude separates religion and economy.[10] He sees in it one source of modern capitalism. Continuing Weber's demonstration, Merleau-Ponty enlarges upon the logic of such an attitude: rational logic, a logic where the "utilitarian" is sanctified and governs the totality of societal relations:

> The terror of man facing a supernatural destiny which he cannot master, weighs heavily on the Puritan's activity in the world, and in an apparent paradox, by having wanted to respect the distance between God and man, the Puritan winds up bestowing dignity and religious meaning on the world of utility and even on the world of comfort, discrediting leisure and even poverty, applying a rigorous asceticism to his use and enjoyment of the world. A complex relation of Being to Absolute forms a precipitate in the Calvinist way of considering worldly goods and is perpetuated there.[11]

The relation to God, conceived and experienced in daily life as a solitary responsibility in the face of the Absolute, leads to a transformation of one's relations to others and to the world. Social relations are no longer characterized by communion, they are conceived in terms of utilitarianism. The world becomes a field for human action, no longer an environment of symbols but a place where one acts:

> Required to renounce the vital alliance we have with time, with others, with the world, the Calvinist carries to its completion a demystification which is also a "de-poetization" and a "dis-enchantment." . . . Absolute anguish can find no remission in a fraternal relationship with the created: the created represents the matter that we fashion, that we transform, that we organize, in order to proclaim God's glory.[12]

We thus have a logical sequence that goes from religious and moral purity to a "dis-enchantment" of the world through a rationalizing of existence. In turn, societal relations are entirely transformed, consequently leading to the solitude of the subject with its corollaries of individualism, the instrumentalizing of relations with others, the gradual disappearance of the symbolic world. The human being's place is henceforward external to others and to the world; he/she is caught in an operating logic of efficiency over communion.

In this perspective, the other is considered and classified in terms of his or her usefulness to society. Practically speaking, this social utility is evaluated on the basis of exterior signs such as skin color and membership in a precise group of origin. Thus conceived, purity offers a criterion for classifying humans. And consequently, the desire for purity winds up in radical segregation.

These kinds of thought systems, the Puritans' as analyzed by Merleau-Ponty or those evoked earlier by Madeiros, belong to history. They describe the symbolic concatenations having governed world visions and behavior for given groups at given times. They provide one key to history and show how it was possible for a long time to conjoin capitalism and racism. At the roots of both can be found the same religious attitude affirming purity. The domination of whites finds therein one of its ideological justifications.[13]

In actual fact, so we are told, things are necessarily less clear-cut, and they have long since evolved. It's fair to admit that if there exists a land of immigration, it is the United States and that the campaign to end slavery was born in Protestant nineteenth-century England. But in attracting our attention to the logistics involved in going from a desire for purity to segregation of the other, by means of rationality and the "de-poetization" of symbols, Merleau-Ponty sheds an original light on one of modernity's figures. Such thought systems take a long time to uproot. Their effects have continued operating throughout all of history, and these logistics still subtly interfere in behavior and decisions. Even emptied of their explicit religious references, these associations of ideas still continue functioning today in language and attitudes, as well as in relations between human groups. This is why the North American continent is divided in two by a line running from Texas to California. South of this line, *mestizaje* is accepted, even glorified. North of it, *mestizaje* is rejected.[14] Today the line is less distinct, and in all the megalopolises of the world, intermixing of peoples continues. But mentalities haven't caught up. Although declared illegal, segregation continues in minds. The WASP mentality, often criticized and deplored, persists and erects subtle barriers between neighborhoods, in schools, or in the workplace. This mentality has escaped the borders of the North American continent and disseminates its effects well beyond the groups it originated with.

Reinvention at Work

Mestizaje comes along and shatters all this. When children are born, no one can say who they'll be, all the more so when ancestries from the four corners of the earth meet within them and what's more, ancestries whose continuity has been lost in the spasms of history. The mestizo child by its mere existence invalidates binary distinctions and oppositions. His or her body literally makes previously unimagined possibilities exist. The mestizo child opens the symbolic world again. Contrary to what de Pauw thought, diversity is not reabsorbed with time; instead, it increases, as the diversity of identities also increases. All heritages, multiplied indefinitely, cross each other in the streets of modern cities, and no population can stake a claim to "purity."

For *mestizaje* transgresses the binary separations discussed above. It revitalizes differences in order to focus on what humans have in common. It makes the arbitrary nature of barriers erected between people apparent. It makes claiming that social differentiations and identities are grounded in nature vain. *Mestizaje* refuses that roles in society be assigned on the basis of an ideology of purity or of "health." It sheds fierce light on the incoherence and hypocrisy in these ways of looking at things, since the child born has a foot in many worlds that law or custom opposes and wants to keep separate. The mestizo child, through its very existence, challenges the established order and the web of symbols justifying it.

The valuation of *mestizaje* in culture bears witness to a profound reversal. "Black is beautiful," Martin Luther King Jr. proclaimed, and all colors are invited to unite, if only in a slogan. This valuation heralds another way of grounding human universality. Not on some alleged biological order like Gobineau desired, but squarely on differences appropriated in a uniquely human way, meaning through law and a freely subscribed social contract, like Tocqueville defended. *Mestizaje* in our multicultural societies is a permanent reminder of how unpredictable the human adventure is and a reminder of how necessary democracy's project is. So then, the intercultural dialogue reveals itself as capable of surmounting bodily spatial and temporal limits, limits that their bodies impose on humans. Intercultural dialogue does not deny the existence of the physical body and its limits by keeping discussion in the realm of aseptic idealism—but it transcends them and fertilizes them. This dialogue plays a pathfinding role toward a new kind of humanity.

In this way a zone is created where interculturalism can be shaped, a zone between the profound, slow-moving energies involved in forging an identity and the desire for democracy's bond. Recognition resides in this zone. For if borders separate, symbols unite. The body, which all humans have in common, can underpin a renewed awareness of human brother- and sisterhood. Desire and violence blend in the body, but are also canalized there into forms of living together. People come together in mourning the dead, whatever their ethnic origins or skin color. Even if the gestures and words expressing them are different, the principal human symbols create a resonance together that touches a chord in our common humanity.

The mestizo is this encounter's privileged locus. Like Inca Garcilaso de la Vega, the son of a Spaniard and an Inca princess, the mestizo has full access, from the interior, to both cultures, to the diverse examples of humanity.[15] In the same way that a child, born to parents speaking two different languages and who is educated bilingually from the start, doesn't need to translate from one to the other. The child inhabits both worlds on an equal footing. He/She needs no intermediary in order to comprehend each world's poetry, with the result that going from one to the other is not laborious. It can be a suffering. It's also creation, invention. Elizondo: "I belonged to two worlds, this offered me more possibilities." Language, imagination, the body are as many escape routes from the binary world. Identity is not reduced to one's appearance but springs from inside, from a fractured universe forced to create its unity.[16] The fracture in identity becomes a fertile spring. The pain remains but the light shines through it. The New World cannot fail to be mestizo.

Language is where reinvention occurs daily. Having escaped from the official circles in continental France, the French language, gaining renewed vitality, picks up more color and rhythms, phrasing and accents that enchant the ear. This is not "bastardization" but a continuation and a renewal of melodies, through the French spoken in Quebec or in Africa or, closer to home, the French sung in rap. Proof is to be found in dictionaries and in literary prizes. It's impossible to draw a line between a pure, fantasized language and the real-life language, full of vitality and future.

Reinvention occurs in the realm of celebrations and music too. Mestizo subversion has been operating for a long time. Reaching the American continent with the slaves from Africa, the rhythms of jazz spread first throughout the Western world and then to the entire planet. Today, raï and other third world melodies are submerging the West and making artistic expression everywhere more exuberant and vigorous, providing bodies with other rhythms and fresh sensations. Celebrations, whether large-scale festivities or more private affairs, imprint decisive choices on our times.

And the nature of celebrations is changing. Commonly shared, grand explosions of joy are mestizo: the 1998 World Cup of Soccer in France is the epitome of this new kind of celebration. But *mestizaje* here is different from the one Octavio Paz evokes. For him, collective popular celebrations in Mexico only mask the solitude of those who have not succeeded in forging their identity. But the communion of bodies on a Champs-Elysées closed to traffic on the evening of July 13, 1998, didn't mirror solitude but a fresh world, different, in the process of emerging, a world in which humanity is at last reconciled and capable of confronting the future together. The "people of celebration" are making their entrance on the territory of the "jaded peoples." The former dance and stimulate the others, who've forgotten how to dance. They liberate forgotten laughter. Along with them come unfamiliar rhythms, sounds, and melodies that blend with "serious music," thus creating unsuspected delights. And thus *mestizaje* shatters the established symbolic systems. It voids the binary systems with their well-ordered symbols and their perfectly disciplined bodies. It reveals other symbolic worlds and makes them sparkle. Surprised individuals discover these symbols vibrating inside them. New universalism, mestizo universalism, universalism of the body, favorably replace the broad smile of *Y'a bon Banania*,[17] the forever-execrated symbol of the universalism of colonies and traders.

Notes

1. Cf. Nathan WACHTEL, *La vision des vaincus*, Paris, Gallimard, 1992. Also Serge GRUZINSKI, *La colonisation de l'imaginaire, Sociétés indigènes et occidentalisation dans le Mexique espagnol*, XVIe–XVIIIe siècle, Paris, Gallimard, 1988.

2. Cabeza de VACA, *Relation de voyage*, Paris, Actes Sud, 1979, pg. 185.

3. Haniel LONG, *La merveilleuse aventure de Cabeza de Vaca, suivi de Malinche*, preface by Henry Miller, Paris, Pierre Jean Oswald, 1970.

4. Cf. Editions *Autrement*, collection entitled *Morales, La Pureté, quete d'absolu au péril de l'humain*, Paris, 1993.

5. François MADEIROS, *L'Afrique et l'Occident*, Paris, Khartaga, 1985, pg. 45 and following:

> Afrique: Aethiops, ainsi étaient désignés les habitants de cette lointaine contrée. C'est un mot d'origine grecque, dont le sens "face brûlée" met en évidence le lien qui est fait entre la couleur noire posée sur une peau d'homme et cette grande terre qui projette du feu en permanence, sans jamais s'éteindre. L'influence de la Chrétienté sur la pensée de l'homme du Moyen Age permet d'imaginer aisément la fonction symbolique de l'Aethiops, au regard de la dichotomie de destin réservée aux hommes sur terre—pur et impur—et dans les cieux—paradis et enfer. Aethiops apparaît donc, dans l'imaginaire, comme la matérialisation des "noirs péchés" qui conduisent en enter où l'on est brûlé.

6. Georges VIGARELLO, "Découvert, toujours pas révélé," in *Le Corps, Le Monde de l'éducation*, num. 260, June 1998, pg. 28.

7. Ibid., pg. 29:

Aucun doute, la veille tradition platonicienne du corps "prison de l'âme" a perdu toute légitimité. Le corps y était doublement rejecté: obscurcissant par la prison des sens toute connaissance certaine pervertissant par l'attrait du plaisir toute morale possible. La pensée vraie était d'abord refus, opposition délibérée au corps, conquête imposée "toute seule, par elle-même sans mélange" pour mieux entre-prendre la "chasse de chaque réalité." (Phédon). Ce qui désignait la conscience en instance souveraine et le corps en résistance redoutée: obstacle sur le chemin du vrai, obstacle sur le chemin du bien. Un partage que reprend à sa manière la tra-dition chrétienne faisant du corps moins un organisme qu'une "chair," celle que doit surmonter toute entreprise d'affranchissement.

8. Julia KRISTEVA, *Etrangers a nous-memes*, Fayard, Paris, 1988, pg. 283:

En vérité il est rare qu'un étranger suscite l'angoisse terrifante que suscitent la mort, le sexe féminin ou la pulsion débridée "maléfique." Est-il pourtant si sûr que les sentiments "poliques" de xénophobie ne comportent pas souvent inconsciem-ment, cette transe de jubilation effrayée que l'on a appelée unheimlich, que les Anglais nomment uncanny, et les Grecs tout simlement . . . xenos, "étranger." Dans le rejet fasciné que suscite en nous l'étranger, il y a une part inquiétante d'én-trangeté au sens de al dépersonnalisation que Freud a découverte et qui renoue avec nos désirs et nos peurs infantiles de l'autre, l'autre de la mort, l'autre de la femme, l'autre de la pulsion immaîtrisable. L'étranger est en nous, nous luttons contre notre propre inconscient—cet "impropre" de notre "propre" impossible.

9. Paul RICOEUR, *Finitude et culpabilité*, volume II, La symbolique du mai, pg. 33 and following:

La crainte de l'impure . . . vis la diminution de l'existence, la perte du noyau per-sonnel," ou encore: "La représentaiton de la souillur se tient dans le clair-obscur d'une infection quasi-physique qui pointe vers une indignité quasi-morale. Cette équivoque n'est pas exprimée conceptuellement, mais vécue intentionnellement dans la qualité même de la crainte, mi-physicque, mi-éthique, qui adhère à la représeantation de l'impur.

10. Max WEBER, *L'Ethique protestante et l'esprit du capitalisme*, Paris, Pion, 1964 (translated from German).

11. Maurice MERLEAU-PONTY, *Les aventures de la dialectique*, Paris, Gallimard, 1955, pg. 22:

La terreur de l'homme en face d'un soft surnaturel dont il n'est pas le maître, pèse de tout son poids sur l'activité du puritaain dans le monde, et par un paradoxe ap-parent, pour avoir voulu respecter la distance de Dieu à l'homme, il envient à charger d'une dignité et d'un sens religieux le monde de l'utilité et même du confort, à discréditer le loisir et même la pauvreté, à porter les riguerus de l'ascèse dans l'usage de ce monde. Dans l'estimation calviniste des biens de co monde, se précipite et se survit tout un rapport de l'être à l'absolu.

12. Ibid., pg. 23:

Sommé de rompre l'alliance vitale que nous avons avec le temps, avec les autres, avec le monde, le calviniste conduit à son terme une démystification qui est aussi une dépoétisation, un désenchantement. . . . L'angoisse absolue ne peut trouver de détente dans un rapport fraternel avec ce qui est créé: le créé c'est la matière sur laquelle on travaille, que l'on transforme, que l'on organize pour manifester la gloire de Dieu.

13. Cf. Martin MARTY, *Righteous Empire, The Protestant Experience in America*, New York, Dial Press, 1970. Also Conrad CHERRY (ed.), *God's New Israel, Religious Interpretation of American Destiny*, Englewood Cliffs, N.J., Prentice Hall, 1971. These two books offer examples illustrating how such a "logics of purity" spread and gained acceptance.

14. Concerning the opposition between the north and the south of the continent, see Vianna MOOG, *Défricheurs et Pionniers* (translated from Portuguese), Paris, Gallimard, 1963.

15. Inca GARCILASO de la VEGA, *Commentaires royaux sur le Pérou des Incas*, Paris, Maspero, 1982 (translated from Spanish).

16. Mexico and the Virgin of Guadeloupe, both Indian and Christian, give us a wonderful example of the reinventing of symbols. Cf. Virgil ELIZONDO, *Guadeloupe, Mother of the New Creation*, New York, Orbis Books, 1997.

17. In France beginning in the twentieth century, Banania was a powdered chocolate breakfast drink whose logo was a broadly smiling African face uttering in faulty French "Y'a bon Banania!" ("C'est bon Banania"—Banania is delicious!). For many children, this advertising image was their first, and often their only, image of Africans, foreigners, others. A rough equivalent in the United States might be Aunt Jemima.

~

CHAPTER NINE

A Memory with a Future

Where is *mestizaje* going? Elusive, always moving; encumbered with the past, it is already in the future. Disrupting membership in clearly identified groups, crossing borders—territorial borders as well as the borders of trends, ideas, and values. Commingling symbols as well as emotions, ritual, or bodies. Where is *mestizaje* leading us? "Us": both individuals who take their identity from it and the others who want nothing to do with it. And "us" also means the groups moving, shifting, existing in that in-between space at the margins of well-defined zones. "Us" refers to the people who want to go unnoticed, to melt into a common anonymity—but that's impossible: faces cannot be erased, the body and its signs exist, and the others read them and reflect back a deformed image. "Us" also means the people who, on the contrary, make being mestizo a source of pride and see in their intermediary position a promise for the future. Where *is* this impossible-to-stop mechanism leading? It's necessary and uncontrollable, a stigma for some, a source of creativity for others. Everyone is affected.

The major cleavages that have always divided our societies are reappearing with *mestizaje*. As we've seen, adopting a position on *mestizaje* is also adopting a position regarding humanity: humanity today, humanity in the future. Fantasizing humanity, or at least one's own group, as pure and sure of its origins, and from there assigning to everyone (to others especially) their place (inferior naturally) leads to justifying all forms of segregation. Despite the heavy price already paid by all the peoples of our planet, the great phantasm of the pure dominating the others continues wreaking its devastation. And there are many ways of considering oneself pure. Ignoring this fact is opening the door to the worst excesses. The only way to counter this risk is to slowly but surely instill democratic values, as Tocqueville proposed. So, where to situate *mestizaje* in relation to the future? Is it a relic, a leftover from other times, fated to disappear once humanity is at long-last mature? Or, on the contrary, is it the hope and the model for the future, advancing toward universal blending, not just biological but cultural too? Visions of *mestizaje* run the gamut from disappearance to grand utopias, from a phenomenon having lost its energy to one exploding with vitality. From total oblivion for what represents after all only one brief moment (the few centuries of colonization) when compared to all of human history, to universal promise for which these same few centuries will have served as painful yet decisive herald.

Vasconcelos, or Cosmic Utopia

A messianic *mestizaje* exists, and José Vasconcelos (1882–1959) is no doubt its most eminent standard bearer. What an extraordinary character this Mexican statesman was, education minister in 1920, renowned author and scholar who, in reaction to the ambient positivism of his times, wanted to propose a philosophy of beauty and spirituality for his country. Among his many books, Vasconcelos has left us a short book of around fifty pages entitled: *La raza cosmica*,[1] the cosmic race. It's a text that wants to be prophetic and whose aim is ushering in the future.

In the very first lines, he states his thesis: "The central idea of the present book is that the world's different races tend to increasingly mix, in the end creating a new human type in which each of the existing peoples has contributed selected characteristics."[2] He then rapidly summarizes human history, or to be more exact his vision of what he imagines this history to be. His aim is to explicate the current state of things, starting with a common origin, proceeding to the diversity of races, their commingling and mutual enrichment through *mestizaje*. He begins with the mythical *Atlantis*, lost continent but also home to the primordial race from which all the others stem, each with their specific wealth and characteristics: Asians and their sense of organization; Africans with their artistic abilities; the Amerindian races which for him are very close to the original race of Atlantis and have preserved all its virtues. And lastly, the Whites, whose mission is to serve as a bridge.

> The White man has brought the world to the point where all types (of men) and all cultures can fuse. The civilization the Whites conquered, organized for our era, laid down the material and moral bases for the union of all men into a "universal fifth race," fruit of the preceding races and transcendence of the entire past.[3]

The two groups that led this evolution, the Saxons and the Latins, that is, the English and the Spanish, began warring in Europe. They exported their conflict to the American continent, and, for example, Napoleon's sale of Louisiana to the Americans represented a setback in this conflict, with the result that suddenly the responsibility of Mexico and Latin America is all the greater. It's a mission "unprecedented in history," reinforced by the fact that in Mexico the Whites and the Indians mixed, whereas the Saxons destroyed the Indians.

At present, for Vasconcelos, we've reached the state of world unification, the "mundo uno" stage, and this is thanks to Spanish colonization which created *mestizaje*, "the first example of racial synthesis on the globe." Being this synthesized race "assigns a responsibility and defines a future." It's a divine mission, and all the signs and factors are favorable: climate as well as natural resources, along with the biological, social, economic, and spiritual factors. What directs the process is "la ley del gusto," the law of desire. It is indeed a different law from the law of science. It is permanent, whereas science changes. This law of desire is the energy and power of love, which for Vasconcelos coincides with Christianity's message.

This process of world unification occurs in three stages. The first stage, material, characterized by war and exalting violence, is the encounter between peoples. The second stage is intellectual or political and founded on reason. The third stage is spiritual or aesthetic and develops creativity and sensitivity to beauty. Education is its underpinning. It's this third stage that is beginning today: "Current circumstances are favorable to the development of interracial sexual relations." For Vasconcelos, this is unhoped-for support for his concept that, lacking a better name, he calls the "future race."[4]

He's not talking about a superior race, and Vasconcelos in passing rejects Darwin as well as Gobineau and Nietzsche. But he concludes: "We thus have present on the American continent all the elements of the New humanity. Only the Iberian part of the continent has the spiritual factors, race and territory, which are necessary to the great enterprise of beginning the universal era of humanity."[5]

Utopia, an unattainable dream no doubt, even if the word *raza* has a broader sense in Mexican than in French and is not limited to its biological meaning. *Raza* refers to the nation, one's land or region, to the group considered a unique and original assembly: the Mexicans, the Mexican people who proudly lay claim to their identity as mestizos. In summary, what is happening in Latin America is seen as auguring, and inaugurating, what awaits all of humanity, since as defined by Vasconcelos, this fusion first of groups, races, and shortly afterward of ideologies and religions, a fusion both biological and spiritual, is the way of the future.

So, is Vasconcelos the anti-Gobineau? Not exactly. He is more of a reverse Gobineau, since from the same presuppositions as Gobineau, he comes to opposite conclusions. Both men are searching for one unique principle that would explain history. Both men try to deduce the future from the past. Both use *race* as the key notion in their thinking. But whereas one, Gobineau, concludes that the processes he sheds light on contain unavoidable degeneration, the other sees progress and a radiant future shining through the filigree of his dream. For even though Vasconcelos gives the notion of race an infinitely broader meaning than Gobineau, it is nevertheless true that he sees it as a notion that can explain everything, even if for him race is not just a question of biology but contains spiritual elements, too. And in the end, his vision leads him to adopt and even reinforce hackneyed stereotypes, classifying the races as more or less advanced, this time not as a function of their distance from a "pure" starting point, but as a function of their aptitude at attaining the proclaimed common horizon. As a result, he declares certain people are more advanced than others! The prejudices over the biology of individuals are replaced here by prejudices over their spiritual dimension, where quality is automatically linked to an ethnic group.

Herein lies the difficulty. We're still in a monist thought system, that is to say, a system that wants to find one unique and universal principle explaining the world. But even enlarged, even made part of Vasconcelos' optimistic and spiritual vision, the concept of race is not suited to the role. Automatic progress doesn't exist, any more than automatic degeneracy does. *La raza cosmica* is a dangerous phantasm!

It was worth taking some time with Vasconcelos' thought. Coming from an esteemed humanist, this thinking enables us to discern the fragile line separating dream from reality. It's true that once these kinds of themes are broached, almost automatically utopia springs up. And with it, danger. The history of Latin America has been marked by these outbreaks of utopia, often with devastating effects. From the very start of the colonial enterprise, weren't the minds of the first Franciscans leaving for New Spain filled with Joachim de Flore and a desire to found the New Jerusalem? On the American continent, utopia accompanies history.[6] Of course, this is not just true of the Americas. All civilizations at one time or another have seen themselves as the saviors of humanity. Utopia, dream, messianism. Reality never ceases contradicting these kinds of recurrent fantasies and reminding us to get our feet back on the ground of the reality of human encounters.

Besides, Vasconcelos' phantasms don't stand up to fact. In an excellent essay, Yves-Charles Granjeat gives us an on-site study of *mestizaje* at work along the border between Mexico and the United States. *Atzlán, Terre vole, terre promise, les peregrinations du people Chicano* (Atzlán, Stolen Land, Promised Land. The Peregrinations of the Chicanos), is the title of his book.[7] It's a case study describing the elaboration of the mestizo myth among the Mexican Americans of the 1960s. Crafted by intellectuals and artists, the story of the mythical origins of the Chicanos echoes in the hearts and minds of millions of immigrants, to whom it offers a discourse of identity. To people deprived of a land all their own, it tells the story of Atzlàn, the primordial homeland of ancestors impossible to know because existing in pre-historic times. Atzlàn is adorned with every virtue. All hopes for the future revolve around it. But in the space between past and future, what remains is deprivation, absence, violence. So only two solutions remain: either give oneself totally up to the nostalgia of a mythical golden age, or chase after a fulfillment and completeness always still yet to come.

Granjeat goes on to show how this kind of never-ending movement continues on and consumes itself. An exile, an identity never secured: "I am he who runs (away)," is how he defines the mestizo. Endless peregrinations, headlong flight, perpetual questing after political or mystical dreams. The result is not Vasconcelos' new messianic race, but an endless roaming where identities and human bonds are lost. Thus Granjeat, proof in hand, debunks all would-be mestizo messianism. It would be impossible to bring a people, an identity, a future into existence grounded in a void like this. By definition, this future is unstable, unbearable. Granjeat has demystified Vasconcelos.

A Profound Reversal

In the end, making *mestizaje* a (perfect) object, the universal key to human history, a messianism destined to save a people or all peoples, leads to emptying it of all substance, of any interest, transforming it into a kaleidoscope of colored paper, an empty shell of a dream. And it leads to missing the point about what *mestizaje* can signify for our contemporary societies. For today the mestizo is not he/she who runs or flees but he/she who "comes." "I want to make this country my country," said a French high school student demonstrating during the autumn of 1998. It's no longer a question of a messianic dream but of an undertaking: the determined effort to give the existence of cultural encounter and the interpenetration of cultures its full importance. If the word *mestizaje* is reappearing, it's as a sign of something that ought to be brought into the open. It doesn't signal a hidden or ignored object, or an object not having assumed its full importance. *Mestizaje* doesn't designate an object but a process, meaning one or several mechanisms of transformation.

If *mestizaje* is a word used in different fields, biological or cultural, without there being any necessary relation between these fields (and contrary to Gobineau's ideas, even less any influence or control of one field over another), it's clearly because it touches on the "how" of how things function and not on the "what" of the nature of things. *Mestizaje* is not a "state." *Mestizaje* is about movement, understood here as the transformation of societal bonds, a process that in the realm of culture has to do with humanity's diversity and universality, individual and group identity, and the violence, more or less present, accompanying this transformation. Once more we come across here the three aspects of culture we noted in the beginning. For each of these points, understanding *mestizaje* as a process, and not as an object, up-ends the word's negative connotations and makes the word a kind of revealing acid for contemporary situations. *Mestizaje* goes from negative, or at the very least from suspect and marginal, to positive. It is a word having to do with the self-representations that human beings forge for themselves. It names, indicates, gives existence to, and thereby transforms the reciprocal relations between humans. The history of recent centuries has shown this process to be one of modernity's effects. It's a process that characterizes a transformation underway, both for individuals and groups.

It's indeed modernity that gave a name and content to *mestizaje*. It's significant that the world *mestizaje*, and along with it all the intellectual modes of classifying human beings according to the characteristics of race, appeared at the dawn of modernity, at the same time as European and colonial expansion. In the presence of the different human beings and the new civilizations discovered, about which fantasizing is no longer possible because they are present in flesh and blood in all their diversity and distinctness, the question arises of humankind's unity and humanity's universality. We are familiar with the debates occasioned by these questions.[8] The idea of humanity as universal, which gains wide acceptance at the time, is nevertheless an abstract idea. Integrating the new arrivals, along with the ever-more tangible diversity that is the consequence of colonization on this universality, will be done using the notion of *mestizaje*. There is a correlation between this notion and modernity's concept of universal humanity. The notion of *mestizaje* enables articulating concrete situations and humanity's abstract universality. Mestizos are human beings, of course, but "mixed." Gobineau simply takes this idea to its extreme and systematizes it. Integration into humanity's fold is accomplished by discrimination among humans, since the decision makers over vocabulary and norms are convinced that their concept of universal humankind is the right one.

This kind of integration-through-discrimination creates a network of borders within a group. Within society, differences are identified and tears appear in the social fabric. These tears are thought unavoidable since they appear as the price to pay—the payment required of others —for membership in the common humanity. This membership is granted but it's a discounted one. As we've seen, color was the sign of this. But dividing lines aren't stable, and the mathematics of color, in a world at the time dominated by mathematics, will vainly attempt to pin them down: proof that the mechanism's core is undermined and that the universalism it claims to champion is suspect. From its vantage point along these shifting boundaries, *mestizaje* reveals the fracture. Like a fault line, *mestizaje* uncovers what underlies social groups and what precisely they try to mask by repeating well-oiled discourses. At this point, classifications stumble, stories of origins skid out of control, and commemorations become derisive or cynical, and there results an abyss, a nonmemory, and fractured identities.

In turn, we get violence, external violence but also the internal wound to one's identity. Whether the issue is the land where one lives, one's own origins, or more broadly one's self-image or the image of ourselves mirrored back by others, the most obvious aspect of mestizo identity is a feeling that something is lacking. All the stories, songs, and poems express this lack or absence, the violence suffered and the revolt it arouses. A geographical border can symbolize this wound to identity, materializing along the ground the fault line running through a person's core and reinforcing it by incarnating memory in the earth, one that is precise, materialized by boundary markers and lines on maps. It is a memory that separates. This is true for groups; the stereotypes about foreigners are an example. This can also be experienced individually, even tragically so, since the mestizo child cannot fully resemble either one of his/her parents. Body, language, physical features, and behavior make the fracture highly visible. The mestizo is rejected by both sides, by all sides. The forms of *mestizaje* are multiplying. Arithmetic can't keep up. Elizondo speaks of a dual *mestizaje*: Spanish/Aztec and Mexican/North American. Others speak of triple *mestizaje*[9] between Cubans, Spaniards, and North Americans. In other words, every time something new appears it's as if the violent seminal encounter from which the mestizo emerged was revived, like an original, sorrowful wound that language has never managed to drain.

So, in the beginning of mestizo existence, violence and fracture are present, causing a break in the continuity that habitually characterizes humanity. Origins become elusive. The time line stops at a wall, the memory of origins runs into a dead end and almost immediately a Herculean effort is begun to bypass this fault line, an attempt to simultaneously overcome it, get it in perspective, and deny its existence. Sometimes *mestizaje*'s violence can be idealized: Vasconcelos sees it in the solicitude of Spanish soldiers for Indian women! Mestizo origins can be refused recognition, in the way some parents do when they forbid their children to speak the language of their ancestors in order to be better "integrated." *Mestizaje*'s original fracture often exists in the form of more or less explicit distress. Historians can of course retrace *mestizaje*'s genesis and development. Nevertheless, when all is said and done, this fracture remains present as a wound. And recognizing where it comes from is not enough to exorcize it because this wound is constantly reopened by language, appearance, behavior that are all reminders of the fact that one is different from the others. Beyond physical traits, this wound is internalized into a feeling of illegitimacy with its attendant shame and guilt. Impossible to admit one's origins. Words attempt denying what features suggest. Integration, held up as a positive value in society, doesn't succeed in masking the tension at the pit of one's stomach, it intensifies it instead. Hence the outbreaks of violence, when the mask suddenly threatens to crack and reveal the original wound. Even if an individual succeeds in making peace with this wound, the others are there on the outside to revive it. Traditional vocabulary and categories of *mestizaje* are daily reminders of this original wound, by underlining that an individual belongs not to the people of the victors but to the vanquished, that he/she was born of a defeat.

But the profound reversal occurring puts this fracture at the center; recognizing it, it becomes the touchstone for the new identity. The violence suffered, the defeat, the fracture are what enable an individual to claim a rightful place in a common humanity, in tangible human universality. And a legitimate place at that. Malcolm X rejected his slave name and adopted "unknown" as his veritable identity.[10] The absence of a name becomes pride in a new name. Words change meaning, and the words expressing marginal status and contempt become the words of legitimacy, sources of pride. Like *Chicano*, or in France *Beur* or *Black* (*Beur* designates a person born in France of North African parents). A group's self-perception is deconstructed, then reconstructed. Empires assigned individuals a place, a role, an identity depending on where they were situated along the scale of colors. Ethnic origins, sex, and religion were characteristics determining this identity, which was devalued compared with the identity of the dominant group. The advent of democracy unlocks the situation by granting individuals citizen status without regard to their particularisms. Sex, religion, ethnic group are no longer elements defining citizen identity. This allows civil society complete freedom regarding how to consider and evaluate differences and discover anew the wealth contained in human differences. Society thus becomes a "rainbow" society, multicolored, where it's no longer to be feared that differences will be transformed into inequality. So, to use Taylor's vocabulary, it's less an issue of "recognizing" clearly identified communities or de facto situations, than it is of creating the conditions for the process leading to a profound reversal. When the fracture, the fault line, differences are made central, they are recognized and consequently a place is made for innovation, newness, novelty. In this way, zones appear where real people can meet and cultures intermix and interact, "mestizo zones," where new identities can emerge.

Nevertheless violence doesn't automatically disappear; however, it is named, recognized, and can consequently be transformed. Past events remain, whatever their degree of violence, but are transfigured. The wound or its scar is present, but the light can shine through. This is achieved through determined effort, whose instrument is the narrative accounts serving to reconstruct memory. All memory is memory of violence, but of a violence crossed through and overcome, radically. Otherwise death would have triumphed: the death of humans and of violence—leaving only a void. Memory, no matter how painful, is proof we are alive, that violence didn't win, that the individual did. Memory can be as painful as a fresh scar, sometimes imperceptible, elusive but present, creating at the core of an individual those zones we don't dare touch, and at a group's core, zones where those never-talked-about subjects are stored. Although never evoked, these subjects are transmitted from generation to generation. They govern conversations and silence, decisions as well as the paralyzing inability to decide or act. It's impossible to move forward carrying so much dead weight. Reconstructing memory enables these subjects to come to the surface and be made present. Along with them, there resurfaces all the associated high feelings, all the long-suppressed violence, but decanted, defused, suddenly emptied of the fears it contained: in short, transfigured. Now the future can open up. Negro spirituals give us an example. They touch the soul and render present for us in the here and now the suffering (which to be truthful nothing can really express or represent) of the men and women whose humanity slavery destroyed. But their voices, thanks to the singers keeping these songs alive today, ring out and continue to affirm hope and the certainty that humanity can triumph over violence.

The fact remains that bringing a fractured identity to the surface involves more than remembering the past or learning about it in books. Only the words of imagination, poetry, songs, can give presence to what will forever escape us. Art is, in this respect, crucial. Reaffirming differences, art blends, assembles, and testifies that harmony is possible and violence transcended. And this time not by applying an abstract universal concept but through the valuation of the multiple, tangible faces sharing in the same human condition. The same words, and *mestizaje* above all, still define the same stakes, but turn them around: abstract to concrete, discrimination to valuation. Memory now liberates the future, it becomes a memory with a future.

The Future's Unpredictable Element

The unprecedented nature of the present situation makes such a profound reversal possible. It's a necessary reversal. The multicultural makeup of our societies increases both the number of groups living in the same territory and the interaction among these groups. The dividing lines between groups, traditions, and cultures are continuously redrawn with still infinite possibilities. Interface along these "border areas" is becoming more frequent. Of course, we're no longer in the presence of compact, well-defined groups, as in the time of colonial empires. What we have here are other forms of living together and interacting, apparently more limited, more localized, yet at the same time involving an increasing number of people. Interculturalism is omnipresent and with it, so are the multiple forms of *cultural mestizaje*.

Consequently, the problems linked to differences, to intermixing, and to the violence that the historical forms of *mestizaje* pushed to an extreme can be seen everywhere. But now, it's precisely *mestizaje* that's pointing to possible solutions to these problems.

Differences, intermixing, violence are in a way what humanity abhors. Both individuals and societies want to contain them, to canalize every social relation so it will involve no risk, to move violence elsewhere in order to contain it and make it the other's problem to deal with. But at the same time, there's no existence worthy of the name unless it's open to the universal, to encounters with others, to risking the unknown. *Mestizaje* is there to indicate a possible path, since it represents for humanity the locus where identities, borders, and individual life choices as well as collective societal choices are ceaselessly called into question. Like a ripple on the surface of water, it runs through groups and societies echoing the jolts that shake them and that they would prefer ignoring, worried, even frightened as they are about what they're going to engender. The profound reversal being experienced invites us, on the contrary, to take a good, square look at them, to see the potentialities contained in multiculturalism open to *mestizaje*.

It's the child who's mestizo, born of parents of different "races," to speak like the dictionaries, born of parents ethnically or culturally different. This is to say he/she is "other" than the parents and will never completely resemble either one. At the same time, the child incarnates the unpredictable "something new" born of the parents' encounter. The same is true of cultures. Let's listen to Elizondo:

> The new identity eliminates neither the original culture of the parents nor the culture of the new country we live in. On the contrary, it enriches both by opening each culture to the possibilities contained in the other. It destroys neither one but it undoubtedly enriches one and the other.[11]

Birth, "something new." It's not merely a question of lovely metaphors since, as we've seen, the intercultural encounter calls into play not only a rationality concerned with organizing and determining but also imagination, the world of symbols and finally, the body too. The child born carries the promises of a world over which the parents have no hold. The child heralds the end of the world that came before.

What's new here is not the "new" of borders newly fixed once and for all, nor the "new" of a revolution imposing a new social order. The pro-found reversal at issue is not the one proclaimed by grand utopian vi-sions. Revolutions, utopias, systems all hit a stumbling block at this point because in one form or another, they all want to determine what the future will be. But it's impossible to determine what the birth of a human being contains and promises. The only sure thing is that, sooner or later, this "something new" will challenge what we considered firmly established.

This is the real reason *mestizaje* arouses so much hesitation and doubt. For by his or her mere existence, the mestizo makes borders relative, interrogates identities and values, challenges the established order.

> Make no mistake: we're definitely in the presence of subversion (a simultaneous toppling of set ideas and values and also a politics of over-turning the established order) when a discourse that's been kept on the sidelines for almost two centuries, cunningly catches up with the central discourse by simple geo-ethnic shift and becomes an integral part of the central discourse in order to give an accounting of the cultural interstice occupied by the modern Mestizo within the Western world.[12]

Subversion of the past, emergence of the future; two sides of the same undertaking. On one side, ideas, values, and institutions that become outdated and constantly have to be readjusted and reformu-lated. On the other side, lifestyles, relationship modes, expressions, and languages ceaselessly appearing and which must be given a place. We move from the side of the intercultural encounter, rich, stimulat-ing, fecund, to the side where the ideas and institutions necessary to any society's survival are organized, implemented, and made to exist. The body, dreams, and the poem of an individual's existence on the one hand; the rationalism of intellect and organizations on the other. The two sides will never mesh, but out of their tension springs move-ment. *Mestizaje* along the confines of cultures revives this tension and encourages movement. In changing register from race to culture, it marks a radical change with regard to violence. It's possible for the former locus of discrimination and inequality to become the locus of a transforming recognition, of universality and of new identities.

And so what *mestizaje* reveals rejoins our common humanity. Our modern societies are increasingly aware that there is no "one way of looking at things," no structure or group into which everyone can be made to fit. There is no such thing as a definitive identity—not for individuals, not for groups. The only thing that exists is the here and now, which it is necessary and important to open to the future. Desiring humanity to stay in one place, whether that place be the sorrow and violence of the past, or a utopia to come, is pronouncing humanity's death sentence. For the past, even atrocious, is past and memory's function is precisely to exorcize its death-dealing residues, in order that the past's vital, creative energies emerge to engender the future. We never stop wanting to define who we will be and what our societies will be like. But this time, short-memoried history should teach us that no representation of the future has the power to make it materialize. However marvelous, it remains a dream. But a dream does have a role to play; it can motivate and give us the energy for the projects of the here and now, a here and now that is a new being, like a child, created by *mestizaje*. None of the ancestries of which it is the fruit can claim to completely control this child, because the very essence of its existence is "otherness." Unpredictable. Unpredictable *mestizaje*. Thus *mestizaje* becomes an integral part of the human condition. *Mestizaje* is a paradigm for humanity.

Notes

1. José VASCONCELOS, *La raza cosmica*, Mexico, Espaza-Calpí, 1948.
2. Ibid., pg. 9.
3. Ibid., pg. 16.
4. Ibid., pg. 10.
5. Ibid., pg. 52.
6. Cf. Jean SERVIER *Histoire de l'Utopie*, Paris, Gallimard, 1967.
7. Yves-Charles GRANJEAT, *Aztlán, Terre vole, terre promise, les peregrinations du people Chicano,* Paris, Off-Shore: Presses de l'Ecole Normale Supérieure, 1989.
8. Cf. Tzvetan TODOROV, *Les morales de l'histoire*, Paris, Grasset, 1991.
9. Cf. Roberto S. GOISUETA, in *Caminemos con Jésus*, New York, Orbis, 1995.
10. *Malcolm X Speaks*, New York, Grove Press, 1965.

11. Virgil ELIZONDO, op. cit., pg. 154.
12. Michel LALONDE, op. cit., pg. 121:

Ne nous y trompons pas: il y a bien subversion (bouleversement à la fois des idées reçues et des valeurs reçues, et aussi politique de renversement d'un ordre établi) lorsqu'un discourse, tenu à l'écart pendant Presque deux siècles, rejoint sournoisement le discourse central par simple déplacement géo-ethnique et s'y installe pour rendre compte de l'interstice culturel investi par le métis moderne à l'intérieur de l'Occident.

Conclusion
A *Paradigm for Humanity*

Paradigm: the word's usual definition signifies model. It comes from the Greek *paradeigma*, which does indeed mean model, architect's blueprint, a painter's or sculptor's model. It's related to the word *deigma*, meaning what is visible, a manifestation or sign of life, but also, what is displayed, indication, supposition, conjecture. In Athens, it referred to the market stand for displaying fruit and vegetables. For Levinas, a paradigm is the "possibility of signifying using a tangible object freed from its history.[1] *Mestizaje* as paradigm: *mestizaje* exhibits, displays, makes visible; it indicates—like an example, artist's model, guiding image, or prototype—what our societies convey, in which direction they are headed, and how. In short, it signifies in which direction humanity is going.

Mestizaje thus carries a meaning for all of humanity. But what meaning? It undulates through humanity as the wave through the ocean, never still, always moving. Its contours are imprecise. There is not one *mestizaje*, but different kinds. Some people use this term in referring to other people they want to set apart. They differentiate by discriminating. Regardless of the explicit content the word evokes, regardless of the place referred to or the groups affected, *mestizaje* is related to the idea of discrimination, of singling out and setting apart. This can be either social or mental discrimination. As a result, the word *mestizo* evokes a fracture in society, a tear in the social fabric that isn't just an issue over assigning differing roles in society's organization but represents a disqualification, an illegitimacy, a situation that shouldn't exist, a betrayal of our common humanity.

To this discrimination corresponds a secret wound in each victim, often unacknowledged, seeming too shameful to admit. As if, once again, that mechanism functions by which the victims are considered guilty and made responsible for their own marginal status, even though they are the first to suffer the associated discredit. At this point, a game of calculated strategy begins: classification, compensation, intimidation. Many become avid players of this game, whose sole motivation is masking, yet ceaselessly aggravating, the alienation at its source.

Our shared humanity now suddenly vibrates. For what human being has no inner estrangement to vanquish? And who has never been trapped in a game of calculation and strategy in order to escape the reality of a situation, in an effort to deny reality, rather than recognize it? But recognition supposes being recognized. Not just legal or political recognition, but a recognition grounded in a mutual exchange of memory and verb. Charles Taylor's notion of recognition needs to be taken this far.

At this point the fracture can be transcended. The existence of a mestizo child is in and of itself proof that a new being is born, can be born, as once a new people were in the New World, with a brand-new chance for generating human relationships and inventing an identity. What originally was associated with rejection is revealed as an illumination. The men and women who have experienced this profound reversal render visible what remains ignored. The mestizo is obliged to confront in his/her own story what remains unacknowledged in other people's stories. The secret fracture of a wounded identity becomes the fulcrum for a new identity.

Mestizaje thus brings to light what composes every human relation: difference, encounter, risk, violence. Ideologies, institutions, symbols must redefine themselves in relation to these basic components. And the future opens up. This future can't be defined in advance. No one can claim to ordain or forbid anything at all to future generations, since these very things will be the fruit of *mestizaje*. Not an idea, but like a child a fruit, a procreation.[2]

Will the word *mestizaje* continue to be used? Maybe it will disappear from our vocabulary. We can indeed hope that the meaning it had in modern times, linking discrimination to "race," skin color, ethnic origin, will disappear. We can hope that the teaching of democratic ideals will gradually shape societies no longer dominated by inequality and contempt. The passage from empires to democracy marked, and still marks, headway in this direction. If discrimination were to disappear, then the word would lose its pejorative connotation and retain only its positive aspects: a testimony to human diversity linked to the universality that manifests itself in this diversity; an identity rich because multiple and open; the permanent dynamics of groups and cultures, exchanging, encountering, procreating. But it's a daily struggle to ensure that the second—positive—meaning predominates. The future of the word is less important than the future of this struggle. Will humanity ever see an end to it? At the very least, we can hope that humanity will succeed in better mastering the violence inherent in this struggle.

What is at stake in *mestizaje* is also at stake in how human beings conceptualize social bonds. From the onset, these bonds are made up of disparities, in other words, differences. Age differences, involving time, between parents who conceive and children who are conceived. Sexual differences separating humanity into "male and female." Differences in ethnic origins, involving space and culture, and differentiating individuals according to the place of their origin on planet Earth. Up until now, the way the social link was managed was to transform the disparities and differences into equality, to create societal models where tradition, religion, even science legitimated the inegalitarian order. Ethnic variety, a wealth for humanity, is thus transformed into inequality, imposing the domination of some over the others. Conceived this way, the social bond cannot fail to be discriminatory. However, the rupture and turning point represented by democracy, which is at the heart of our societies and what they are striving toward, leads to giving human diversity a different status. This does not mean considering this diversity some kind of homogenized state in which nothing is distinct or distinguishable. There will be no cultural "caféaulaitisation," were we even to suppose that it is biologically probable. Likewise, there will be no universal melting pot, if by this we mean a vast can of paint where all the colors are combined, resulting in a nondescript tone.

Other images have begun to appear: the *rainbow* used in this book, or the *united colors* of advertising fame. Elizondo's favorite image is the "*stew pot*," an image that speaks of mixture, slow exchange of flavors, necessary heat. And of time, too.

Mestizaje unfolds at the speed of individual adventures, but also at the speed of the collective violence and large movements and shifts in population making up history. Having long occurred without our countries' being conscious of it, *mestizaje* had the relative immobility and the power of geological phenomena, and like tectonic plates, transformed society right under our feet without our being aware. Suddenly, in a few decades, the situation altered because of economic pressure and the economy's need for immigrant labor. It altered because of wars, too, which continue displacing populations in proportions rarely before seen, and through technology, enabling us to go from one point to another on the planet in a few hours and informing us in real time. As a result, what used to be marginal, imperfectly grasped, or too slow to be perceived except through catastrophes, becomes our daily fare. And the other person at the remotest point on Earth becomes a close relation. The different speeds of time are telescoping, and the time of *mestizaje* is becoming our ordinary time. No longer the slow time, over generations, but the immediate time of cultural exchanges. Will the result be the "Steel Cage" proclaimed by Max Weber, enclosing humanity in technology's binary logic?[3] Or will the element of unpredictability inherent in *mestizaje* introduce some play, introduce its play, into the confinement of the new technological empires that are augured here and there?

Confronted with what is taking shape, our thought categories need to be constantly readjusted. The advent of democracy rendered inoperative the concepts of clan or ethnic group that had long structured our societies. Disconnecting democracy from ethnic ties seems today to be self-evident. This is nevertheless periodically threatened by a resurgence of particularisms. Thus the task is never finished. New and unforeseen situations multiply, and the challenge takes on a new dimension. It's becoming increasingly urgent to renovate our thinking on the democratic bond, re-examine the issues at their roots, and give some fresh thinking to the underpinnings of how to live together in a shared territory and to the reasons why we should want to be active, willing parties to a social contract. Not a contract representing just some general framework for shared existence, but an ongoing, daily process of elaboration in close touch with groups and situations: a permanent exchange in which memory is shaped, violence gotten through, society woven.

This is where the notion of *recognition* comes into play. Not recognition limited to a manifestation of good will or diplomacy, but recognition as a basic requirement for forging the democratic bond. However, this notion must necessarily be taken to its limit and made to include what, for each person, constitutes the unique and inalienable aspects of his or her identity. This notion must be made to also include what, in any given place, the human beings and the cultures have signed together, the democratic pact to procreate/create.

Geography once again becomes an important factor. Not as a place left behind, or a nostalgia for the ancestral land, not frozen in the past, but as a territory where multiple heritages converge and together weave the future. This involves looking forward, and less backward toward a mythical past, immutable traditions, or an illusory purity, a danger inherent in all nationalism or all fundamentalism. It means looking ahead instead, toward the possibilities that spring from human encounters, from inevitable *mestizaje* in all its forms. Thus we are not at the end of history. On the contrary, we are facing history's perpetual renewal, the "something new" constantly, indefinitely recreating itself. Unpredictable, just like the continuous flow of humans commingling and giving birth to other humans, with the resulting emergence on the face of the Earth of a wide variety of societies and cultures. *The time of mestizaje* is today.

Notes

1. Cf. *Encyclopaedia Universalis*, article "Paradigm."

2. François LAPLANTINE, Alexis NOUSS consider *mestizaje* to be an ethics of existence offering a "dynamics of becoming" particularly suited for inspiring the contemporary world. Cf. *Le métissage*, op. cit., pg. 111.

3. Max WEBER, op. cit., pg. 246.

Index